Frank Freidel, a specialist on the history of American political institutions, has been Professor of History at Harvard University since 1955. For the academic year 1955-56 he was Harmsworth Professor of American History at Oxford University, and in 1959-60 he was a Fellow at the Center for Advanced Study in the Behavioral Sciences at Stanford. Professor Freidel is currently at work on a projected nine-volume biography of Franklin D. Roosevelt, three volumes of which have been published. His other writings include *Francis Lieber: Nineteenth Century Liberal* (1947) ; *The Splendid Little War* (1958) ; *America in the Twentieth Century* (1960) ; *A History of the United States* (1958), co-author; *The Golden Age of American History* (1960), editor ; and *Builders of American Institutions* (1963), co-editor.

THE NEW DEAL
and the American People

edited by FRANK FREIDEL

A SPECTRUM BOOK
Prentice-Hall, Inc.
Englewood Cliffs, N.J.

Current printing (last digit) :

13   12   11   10   9

Copyright © 1964 by Prentice-Hall, Inc., Englewood Cliffs, N.J.
*All rights reserved. No part of this book may be reproduced in
any form, by mimeograph or any other means, without permission in writing from the publishers.* Library of Congress
Catalog Card Number: 64-15215. Printed in the United States
of America. C
P 61241

For Charles Robinson Freidel

CONTENTS

Introduction

One of the more interesting challenges to the student of history is to view a familiar scene from a fresh perspective. He may, if he is fortunate, discover new relationships and significance that will give additional meaning to what seemed all too well-known. It is the purpose of the readings that follow to lend such a perspective to the New Deal. Usually it has been viewed by focusing upon President Roosevelt and his associates, or upon his critics, or upon the New Deal agencies and institutions. All of these enter in greater or lesser degree into these readings, but their special focal point is the American people. How were they affected by the New Deal and how did they react to it? As limited a collection as this can do no more than cover a few of the high points in the range and time-span of the New Deal;

there are of necessity many omissions. But these pieces are intended to provide some impressions of reactions between the spring of 1933, when Anne O'Hare McCormick sensed the widespread pressure upon those in Washington to enact a New Deal program, to the aftermath of the 1940 election when Samuel Lubell found a vast urban electorate enjoying the benefits of the New Deal and endorsing its ideology. And they illustrate the attitudes (more often studied) of those alarmed by the New Deal.

Much of the reaction of the public was based upon the depression, and the New Deal for millions of people was above all a response to intolerable living conditions—both through improvement of these conditions and through reform to prevent their return. For many the New Deal brought little except hope, but for many others it did indeed seem to bring substantial improvement. As a result of the massive federal intervention upon behalf of the economic welfare of the general public, expectations of government aid changed drastically and, it would seem, permanently. Yet, as one reads Richard Neuberger's remarkable report on public misunderstandings of the Supreme Court struggle of 1937, one wonders how well informed the American people were in their opinions of the New Deal, except as it touched them personally. There was real necessity behind the efforts of the Social Security Board and state welfare workers to educate the public to the meaning and scope of the Social Security Act. Among both supporters and denigrators of Roosevelt there was much more emotional feeling than hard-headed factual knowledge of over-all New Deal programs upon which to base their reactions. Perhaps the difference was that the people about whom Marquis Childs wrote in "They Hate Roosevelt" felt they were worse off (when materially they might have been better off), while the urban voters Samuel Lubell interviewed knew for a certainty they were better off (because of the ways they or their families had been tangibly aided). For all these people, what they themselves felt or experienced was more important than their understanding of complex issues and institutions in Washington. And for those of a generation later, well versed in the over-all patterns of the New Deal, many of whom did not personally experience it, these readings may be of value in a different way, by providing glimpses of the New Deal as it functioned among the American people.

The Excitement of the Hundred Days

✔ **1. Anne O'Hare McCormick senses the popular impetus for a New Deal.** Visitors in Washington during the first hundred days of the New Deal, as indeed observers throughout the country, felt the powerful public pressure behind the New Deal program. One of the most perceptive of these observers, Anne O'Hare Mc-Cormick, who customarily wrote from Europe for *The New York Times,* analyzed the national mood of May 1933. *Anne O'Hare McCormick, "Vast Tides that Stir the Capital," The New York Times Magazine (May 7, 1933), 1-2, 19. Copyright © 1933 by The New York Times Company. Reprinted by permission.*

WASHINGTON

Wherever you go in Washington today you come upon crowds of people. All day they wait in long queues outside the public galleries of Congress. Or they huddle in little groups in the corridors of the Capitol, in the corridors of the State Department, in the White House waiting rooms, around oddly casual dining rooms in the milling lobbies of hotels. Always they are eager, anxious; always they are talking. The place hums and buzzes and quivers with talk. That Dome of Thought on the Hill, where an ever-expanding nation has so long and perfunctorily cerebrated, is not only subdued, a shorn Samson that cannot even shake the roof; it has become but one of many parliaments. The visitors who swarm there now go mostly to hear the echoes of what goes on in the White House or in the executive departments.

The talk is all echo, everywhere the same, yet in these reverberations there is nothing perfunctory. They are vivified by a strong undercurrent of wonder and excitement. You feel the stir of movement, of adventure, even of elation. You never saw before in Washington so much government, or so much animation in government. Everybody in the administration is having the time of his life. So they say, and so you perceive as you watch the new officials, often young, often inexperienced in politics, settling into this great business of national reconstruction. They dash from conference to conference, from hearing to hearing, briefcases bursting with plans and specifications. They are going somewhere, that is plain, and with such momentum and élan that they take the world in the same stride with which they set about reorganizing agriculture, reflating the currency, reforming the structure of business and industry.

The atmosphere is strangely reminiscent of Rome in the first weeks after the march of the Blackshirts, of Moscow at the beginning of the Five-Year Plan. But in those old capitals the high tension and the ferment seemed forced—imported stimulants for which there was no native appetite. Here the rush and excitement are as natural as light and air. It is a little as if at last America had marched on Washington, so that for the first time the capital feels like the center of the country. Or, better, as if the pioneer who became the go-getter, balked in his go-getting, had turned back to discover a forgotten frontier, and was beginning to transfer his energies from revolutionizing industry to revolutionizing government. Consciously or unconsciously, the setting has been made ready; the new capital built by Mr. Hoover presupposes just such a highly centralized, all-inclusive government as is now in the making.

That difference, however, is not the really significant distinction between this and other revolutionary capitals. In all the rest the social and political edifice was changed to fit a theory. Someone arrived with a dogma and imposed it by force until it was modified and overcome by facts. Here the facts themselves are the motive force. There is no theory, nor much volition, in the American movement. It is almost fortuitous, as automatic in producing a new model as is the conveyor system in the Ford factory. If we are going through a process of conversion—and no one doubts that we are—it is not a change of mind or a change of heart but merely a change in our circumstances.

Upheavals elsewhere, moreover, have been signalized by seizures of power. All the dictatorships we observe from afar, and by now they are a common sight, have been forced on people against their will, or at least against the will of large and unhappy sections of the population. Here it can be said that the pressure is on the other side; something far more positive than acquiescence vests the President with the authority of a dictator. This authority is a free gift, a sort of unanimous power of attorney. There is a country-wide dumping of responsibility on the Federal Government. If Mr. Roosevelt goes on collecting mandates, one after another, until their sum is startling, it is because all the other powers—industry, commerce, finance, labor, farmer and householder, state and city—virtually abdicate in his favor. America today literally asks for orders.

Among all the phenomena on the landscape, viewed from any angle, none is more striking than the reversal of the traditional relation between the country and the capital; for once Washington is the center of activity and the states beyond are passive, waiting for direction. Here is the stage, scene of a performance partly rehearsed, partly prompted by events; the nation is like a vast audience, hanging on to their seats to see what happens.

Three visitors met by chance one evening not long ago in the lounge of a Washington hotel. They came from places far apart, each bent on business of his own, each expecting to find the capital remote from the "realities" with which he dealt. The first was from New York. As director of a great relief agency, he had been immersed for months in the bitter problems of the unemployed. "From here," he said, "New York looks almost segregated. The sense of emergency is so much keener here that I feel as if we had not realized how near the brink the country was; as if on Manhattan Island we but dimly guessed what was going on in the United States, what's going on now."

The second visitor was a manufacturer from the Middle West, come with other manufacturers to find out just what the thirty-hour-week bill means. He was meek, willing to "go along," but bewildered, and what most bewildered him was the docility of his colleagues. "Everywhere," he reported, "they are the same as they are at home, not knowing what it's all about, apologizing for asking questions, but whipped in advance, agreeing to a revolution as casually as if it were just the next step forward. And here that's what it seems."

The third visitor was a Frenchman, a member of M. Herriot's party. "I can hardly believe this is the same Washington I saw three years ago," he remarked. "More than in Europe, I feel here as if I were living in a historic moment. It is a kind of conjunction, I think, of a national mood and a man who expresses it. You who live here have no idea how palpable to a foreigner is your spirit of unity in change. It is as actual as an event. To me it is an event of the highest importance."

It is impossible to interpret what transpires in Washington without reference to this national mood. The action and interaction of the mind of the country with the governing mind explain many things otherwise inexplicable. It is not of their own will that so many Republican members of Congress vote with the majority, nor is it for party loyalty only that the Democrats who grumble in private hew to the line when the roll is called.

That little argument and hardly more than a score of votes could be mustered in the Senate against legislation without precedent in scope and power—the farm bill, for instance, with the inflationary amendment permitting the President to reduce the gold content of the dollar by 50 per cent—represents neither conviction nor yet sheer surrender of function on the part of the legislative body.

The tremendous changes we are enacting are not the result of conviction anywhere, and no one who has watched this Congress voting yes to every administration measure can think of it as an assembly legislating a revolution. Yet that is what it is doing, prodded not so much by the President, who so far has not been obliged to crack the whip in a single instance, as by the same force which pushes him on, too, sometimes, one feels, beyond his intention, faster and further than he meant to go.

This almost involuntary impetus comes from the people. President Roosevelt has a sixth sense for popular reactions. Also he is the kind of man to whom people talk frankly, to whom strangers write freely. Every day he receives hundreds of letters from obscure citizens in all parts of the country. It is amazing how many Americans are moved to offer advice, suggestions and criticism to the President, particularly to this President. Most of these letters require no answer, but they are put in his "bedtime folder" and he runs through them every night or early in the morning. Like Mrs. Roosevelt, the President has a horror of being isolated in the White House. To a guest who sat near him during a motion picture of the campaign trips, showing the throngs of people at every stop, he said: "That's what I miss here—the crowds."

That is what one feels behind Roosevelt—the crowds. To one who has lived in Washington through this "tremendous entrance," to borrow M. Herriot's quotation from Walt Whitman, it is clear that what distinguishes this administration is that it is fresh from the people, in touch with the desires of the multitude. The impression is strengthened if you check up by making an excursion out into the heart of the country, to Detroit or Dayton or Sioux City, any typical industrial town or farming center. Then you perceive that the sense of emergency that moves the government is only the intensification, perhaps the dramatization, of the mood that grips the nation.

The United States has been brought to Washington, the United States in a mood of crisis, a quiet people, peaceable, orderly, very sure it can't stay down, but more dependent on government than it has ever been in its history and demanding omnipotent gestures from government, as many as are necessary to get the machine in motion.

In his present temper the American is not in the least afraid of experiments. He is not thinking of the remote consequences of his emergency demands. In general he does not like dictators; he would not endure the strong-arm methods of Mussolini; he would destroy with laughter the shrill hysteria of Hitler; a Stalin shut up in a Kremlin would be a very unpopular Czar out in Iowa. But he wants action, the immediate action promised by Mr. Roosevelt in his inaugural address and no lobby ever exerted so much pressure on Congress as the people now bring to bear to induce the President to use all the executive authority he can command.

I suppose we have never had a President as powerful as Mr. Roosevelt is at this moment. In a century of growth and change we have not found it necessary to enlarge the frame of government as much as it has been extended in the past sixty days. Not only does the present occupant of the White House possess more authority than any of his predecessors, but he presides over a government that has more control over more private activities than any that has ever existed in the United States.

Consider only the fields in which the Chief Executive has been granted an actual overlordship. The banking bill gives him control of the banking system; under its authority the government has already stopped runs on sound banks and tied up about $5,000,000,000 of deposits in banks it declares not sound enough to reopen. It has placed an embargo on gold exports and taken us definitely off the gold standard. The economy bill enables the Executive to proceed to a complete reorganization of the Federal Government. The farm bill with its amendments practically puts the largest industry in the country under his management. It permits commodity price-fixing and inflation of the currency by any one or all of three drastic methods to be employed at his sole discretion.

The billions allotted to refinance farm and home mortgages, added to the enormous sums loaned to banks and industry by the Reconstruction Finance Corporation, make the United States Government the biggest and most powerful lending agency in the world. The railroad bill, taken together with the authorization to start the huge scheme for the development of the Tennessee Valley, goes measurably in the direction of nationalization of public services.

In addition, pending or proposed, we have a public-works program providing a large government investment in self-liquidating projects. We have reforestation camps under army control, probably a permanent expedient for keeping unemployed youth out of mischief. We have a bill for government regulation of the sale of securities. We have beer, the beginning of the end of prohibition. We have seen the exit, almost without a whimper, of the veterans' lobby, and thus have banished at a stroke the two most powerful political influences of the postwar period. We have adopted the principle, opposed through the whole Hoover administration, of direct Federal relief wherever needed.

Most important of all is the grandiose plan advanced for the organization and coordination under a government board of control of all branches of industry. This envisages a federation of industry, labor and government after the fashion of the corporative state as it exists in Italy.

Even in this brief summary one is dazed by the dimensions of this program, enacted or ready for enactment in the short space of two months. Seen whole, however, it does not appear so inconsistent as did the individual measures as they issued hot, sometimes half-baked, from the hopper. The strictly deflationary measures, such as the cuts in pensions, salaries and government costs and the closing of banks, are surgical measures for chronic tumors in the political and financial systems. The inflationary measures are strong, perhaps dangerous, stimulants to recovery. Whether they work or not, whether the savings effected by the right hand are squandered by the left, it is clear that the unhealthy growths had to be pruned away before progress could be made in any direction.

But that is not all. The administration is not only moving in two directions at once in the domestic field; it charts two opposite roads in world policy and proceeds to follow them both. Mr. Roosevelt drafts tentative plans for a possible state of economic isolation in which the United States will sustain itself and as far as possible contain itself. At the same time he has spent one month out of his two in conference with the representatives of other governments.

In a magnificent effort to turn back the tides into their natural channels, he has dramatically placed himself at the head of the world. He does not ask for a mandate as an international dictator, welcome as such a governor might be to a distracted planet, but if he gets the authority he wants from Congress—to drive trade bargains, to negotiate the best deals he can get and make on war debts—he would be in position to exercise almost as much power abroad as he wields at home. Already it is evident that this government is taking a new line in foreign policy, employing a more aggressive and realistic technique. More, it begins to look as if under the Roosevelt direction the whole world inclines toward the same line.

The observer in Washington today cannot be just an observer. Inevitably he is caught up in the whirl of the drama. He has to read while he runs, but even to the runner certain signs are plain. You see here, for instance, besides all these new laws and powers, any number of other things, new portents. They are mixed with old things, it is true, confused in motive, not too clear or pure in purpose. You see an unconventional, non-political sort of Cabinet, chosen partly for reasons of strictly personal loyalty, but partly, too, because they compose into a new type of governing mind, receptive and flexible. After two months you see most of the local political patronage withheld and Hoover appointees still in some of the most important subsidiary posts. Again, this is partly strategy—a club to drive through a legislative program in the shortest possible time; but mostly it is because there is so much business more urgent than appointing postmasters.

The tightening of authority coincides with a relaxation in the atmosphere, a simplification of administrative procedure, a fade-out of forms and precedents, which convinces you that, whatever this is, it is not what people mean elsewhere when they speak of dictatorship. The academic mind, so called, is pretty much in evidence. Professors are planted at important points in the Departments of State, Agriculture, Commerce and the Treasury; they are among the President's friends and close advisers. "A bunch of amateurs," say the old-timers; but why a professional student of politics or history or economics should not be a better counselor on problems of government than the student of law, the real estate salesman or the banker is difficult to see, particularly after our recent experience with the fond illusions of "practical" men.

The feminine mind is more in evidence, and this not only because the First Lady has a mind of her own and a wide interest in public affairs or because women occupy places in the government they never held before. Rather it is that the women of the administration, like their husbands, are of a new political generation—a little younger, less traditional, less social in the narrow sense, more social-minded. No change is more marked than the transposition into another key of the whole scale of official society. Led by the White House, the Washington that has been growing stiff and in recent years formal, more like a European capital, has gone American again; but very late-American, expressing the mood and mind and manners of a time of transition.

It all works into a new pattern. All the changes come back in the end to that curious community I have spoken of between the mind of the President and the mind of the people. "Let's try something else!" might be the motto of this administration. "Let's try something else!" is the almost unanimous sentiment of America at this moment. Certain sections of the populace are troubled by the idea of inflation. Others have been uneasy as to how a possible six-hour day would affect their business. Millions are still distrustful of all banks and all investments. But nobody, not even Senator Glass, is really terrified by the changes proposed by the President. For two months the country has hardly breathed a protest, though its situation has not basically improved since Inauguration Day, lest a breath should interrupt the progress of the program of "bold experimentation."

Nobody is much disturbed by the idea of dictatorship. Mr. Roosevelt does not fit into the popular conception of a dictator, and there is a general feeling that he collects powers as he collects opinions—to be ready for emergencies rather than with the intention of using them. The people as a whole trust the discretion of the President more than they trust Congress. It is not too much to say, in fact, that the executive authority derives from a kind of mass decision of the American will—one of those sudden motions or emotions of the genius of a people which in critical moments serves as a kind of compass to right its course.

Perhaps President Roosevelt is inventing a method to make democracy work. At any rate, here is a new kind of rule—what might be described as the permissive dictatorship, evolved in a few weeks by a concert of powers: The President, the people, the tyranny of events.

Relief: An Urgent and Enduring Problem

2. **A social welfare executive appraises relief programs to 1935.** New Deal relief programs were varied and complicated; they brought into being large corps of trained social workers whose careers came to center upon administering aid to the needy and, whenever possible, enabling them to obtain employment. Paul L. Benjamin, Executive Secretary of the Council of Social Agencies of Buffalo and Erie County, surveyed for social workers in the spring of 1935 relief programs up to the establishment of the Works Progress Administration, and analyzed some of their effects upon the people dependent upon them. *Paul L. Benjamin, "Unemployment and Relief," The Family (May 1935), 67-71.*

11

Reprinted by permission of the Family Service Association of America.

The urgent need of millions upon millions of Americans when the New Deal began was to obtain immediate succor—food, clothing, shelter. State and local relief administrations and private charity were unable to meet the burden of unprecedented unemployment and suffering. Federal loans late in the Hoover administration were only a temporary palliative. Only the federal government seemed to have sufficient taxing and borrowing power to provide families at the end of their resources with a minimum living standard. Thus it was that although President Roosevelt had pledged during his campaign that he would cut governmental expenditures drastically in order to balance the budget, during the New Deal he signed measures pouring billions of dollars into relief programs. "If starvation and dire need on the part of any of our citizens make necessary the appropriation of additional funds which would keep the budget out of balance," Roosevelt had also said during his campaign, "I shall not hesitate to tell the American people the full truth and ask them to authorize the expenditure of that additional amount." He always placed human needs ahead of a balanced budget—but the problem of relief continued to be critical.

Queen Elizabeth is dead but the poor relief system which bears her name still walks abroad like a troubled spirit. The time has come to lay her ghost. Persistently, all along the line, we must press for a revision of poor laws and a revamping of a system which has outlived its usefulness. In the past we have sought to evade the consequences of antiquated methods by carving out of poor relief certain groups for special treatment—such as the aged, the widowed, and the blind.

It was this ramshackle, creaking wain in which we trundled into the depression. One of the reasons for the pressing into service of emergency vehicles and the building of new ones was the inability of such a mode of transportation to carry the increasing and stupendous load. The past few years, however, have made it clear that we need a modern welfare authority from the federal government down to the counties in the hinterland of America.

During the past few years our steps have been stumbling and uncertain. The first winter we tried to cope with the then "emergency" through the instrument of organized public and private agencies. But the need increased. Various emergency measures were tried. Citizens' Committees were started. President Hoover launched the Emergency Committee for Employment in November, 1930, which acted as a national clearing house. The following winter saw an increase in private relief funds, public subsidies, and the development of work relief. Then state aid was inaugurated. New York State stepped forth with the Temporary Emergency Relief Administration in September, 1931. In 1932-33, after bitter and contentious debate (how like shadow-boxing the opposition now appears!) the federal government took the spot-light with loans through the Reconstruction Finance Corporation, and finally the Federal Emergency Relief Administration, in May 1933, assumed the dominant role in the relief picture.

Various experiments were tested. The most spectacular was the Civil Works Administration, an attempt to combine employment with the administration of relief. In spite of the political skullduggery which accompanied it in some places, it did give a thrust to employment. To thousands of dejected unemployed the chance at work came like rain to a parched land.

Several lessons emerged. It became evident that "dust-pan relief" is no substitute for a job. Men want work. Work and relief mix no better than do oil and water. C. M. Bookman, formerly special assistant to the Federal Relief Administrator, from his months of close-range experience came to the conclusion that "funds designed to increase consuming power should be administered through agencies of government where the public expects work to be done on an efficiency basis." Mr. Bookman favors two kinds of work programs: one to be handled by a regular agency of government, as an engineering department, and the other by a relief agency, "primarily as social therapy." But perhaps most essential is the fact that work should be worth doing.

The Size of the Problem

The monthly Bulletin on Social Statistics of the Federal Children's Bureau and the releases of the FERA have given us a running summary of the colossal nature of the relief job. Single districts in some cities now have more families under their charge than the entire city had previous to 1930.

In 1933 approximately twenty-five times as many cases as in 1929 were aided per month in urban areas of the United States through general relief administered by public agencies. In December 1934, there were 19,018,503 persons—as constrasted with 11,086,598 in January 1934—receiving relief from a public agency in the continental United States. Transients were not included. An unemployment relief census made by the Federal Emergency Relief Administration in 1933 revealed that a third of all those receiving relief were concentrated in the States of New York, Pennsylvania, Ohio, and Illinois. Further, three-fourths of all persons receiving relief resided in urban areas.

The government is now proposing to substitute mainly a work program (with probably a means test) for direct relief and, as a spokesman has expressed it, "to quit this business of relief." Donald R. Richberg, the director of the National Emergency Council, stated recently that "the direct, dole relief is expensive and unsatisfactory." Of course, more work for the unemployed should be applauded. But convincing testimony was presented at the Washington meeting of the American Association of Social Workers to the effect that a huge relief task will still remain to be done. Caution should therefore be expressed against the scrapping of all direct relief, even though we agree with the condemnation of a situation which makes a gigantic relief fund necessary. Homer Folks, secretary of the New York State Charities Aid Association, has buttressed this point of view with the opinion that relieving a need "is enormously less demoralizing than that the need should continue unrelieved."

As might have been predicted, the percentages of relief funds contributed by local communities sharply decreased when the federal reservoir was tapped. The proportion contributed by state funds increased.

Concomitant with this shift has come more and more direction in local relief policies on the part of state and federal authorities. He who pays the piper can call the tune. The advocates of such interference assert that there has been less skullduggery than if local political sachems had access to relief chests. The opponents declare that it has been carpet-bag rule.

Effects of Unemployment

Five years of unemployment of a catastrophic nature have given us direct and convincing evidence of the searing and blighting effect of loss of job upon personality, health, and family life.

In the recent study of the effects of unemployment upon family life made by a committee of the Family Society of Philadelphia, health breakdown directly traceable to unemployment was evident in a large number of the families studied.

One of the consequences of the depression has been "unemployment shock," the twisting and warping of personality resulting from long months of penurious relief with no cash to spend and from pounding the asphalt searching for a job. An unemployed industrial engineer said to me several days ago, "Yesterday my little girl asked me for ten cents to buy a tablet for school. I didn't have it. What could I tell her?"

A summary of the report to the Committee on Economic Security on Child Welfare in a General Program of Social Security shores up our impression that unemployment has also had a deleterious effect upon child life. This recent report points out that "about 7,400,000 children under 16 years of age are in families receiving unemployment relief—representing about 40 per cent of the total number of persons on relief." The report states: "Those engaged in the administration of relief and others having an opportunity to know the problems at first hand are deeply impressed by the gravity of the health, educational, employment, and social problems of the children and young people in relief families and in families on the borderline of relief."

Dr. Louis I. Dublin and Bessie Bunzel, in their recent study of homicides in the United States, came to the conclusion that deprivation and want are nurturing soil for the criminal. Lack of affection and security in early childhood have been the life pattern of many criminals. The resulting feelings of inferiority and jealousy express themselves in striking out against society.

For long years to come we shall be dealing with the social costs of unemployment—of stunted children, embittered and crushed men, women worn and aged before their time, seared and abraded personalities. Social workers will need rare patience, skill, and insight to help maimed human beings struggle back to respect and belief in themselves. Only unusual competence, the best of training, and deep human understanding will be equal to the challenge.

Emerging Problems

A warm controversy has raged around work relief. Its proponents point out that men want work and not a "dole"; that work relief satisfies the desire of men to earn their bread by the sweat of their own hands. They point to the morale-giving values in work itself. They also assert that a community has something in return for its huge relief expenditures when men work out their relief.

The opponents reply that home relief is less expensive than work relief, and how are we going to pay this relief bill anyway? They also claim that the morale values are a delusion. Sir William Beveridge believes that work relief is at best a poor substitute for a job. He states: "Relief work has proved not a happy but a disastrous combination. It generally implies something that degrades the name of work and disregards the principles of relief."

On the other hand, Russell H. Kurtz, of the Russell Sage Foundation, a close student of unemployment relief methods, says in a letter: "It is my opinion that work relief should be improved and extended rather than abolished. As much of it as possible should be pushed over into the field of public works; but to whatever extent able-bodied men and women are then left on the relief rolls, they should be given work. Have all the sound work projects been exhausted in America? Not if we are willing to put more money—including larger local appropriations—into materials."

We probably need to adjust our notions about work. "Work for the night is coming when man's work is done" was the pabulum of our youth. Perhaps a different kind of nourishment is more palatable in a period of great social, economic, and cultural change. Does standing by the moving automobile belt all day long and performing only one simple operation have any real value in it for the man doing it? Where are the creative values in a machine age? Is painting a sunset less worthwhile than fabricating some new gadget? What are the psychological values in work anyway? Is work relief a rule-of-thumb procedure, or does it take into consideration these subtle and inchoate intangibles?

In the opinion of the AASW Committee on Current Relief Problems there are basic objections to mixing work and relief. These are:

(1) Making public employment available only to relief recipients looses a flood of new applications on the relief intake office.

(2) Unemployed persons who wish to avoid relief are penalized for their fortitude in the face of misfortune.

(3) Wage standards are inevitably apt to be compromised toward the work-for-relief level.

(4) Inefficiency in selection and prosecution of projects is more likely to be tolerated than if the work authority were entirely divorced from the relief authority.

The committee states emphatically that, in its opinion, the only solution to the dilemma rests "in the provision of a works program large enough to employ all who wish work, regardless of relief status."

Another issue—production of goods for use rather than profit—has faced vigorous opposition from business interests. The Federal Surplus Relief Corporation has processed great quantities of farm products for the use of the unemployed. Mattresses have been made on a stupendous scale. Factories operated by the unemployed in Ohio are busily making a variety of things. One relief official in New York State recently received five carloads of beef-broth from Washington. One point of view was tersely expressed by David C. Adie, commissioner of social welfare for New York State, who said: "I don't believe in running the economic structure to give people work when it comes through the welfare structure."

On the other hand, some are convinced that the unemployed should be allowed to make things for themselves. They assert that the unemployed tailor who fashions a suit for another unemployed man which he wouldn't otherwise have is not interfering with the normal production of goods by private industry.

The sharpest controversy, of course, has been in connection with the recently announced intention of the federal government to withdraw from the relief field. In response to that intention the social workers assembled in Washington were of the opinion that the government cannot leave the relief partnership without serious results. So long as widespread unemployment is a part of the American scene, so long will the federal government have an implicit responsibility for succoring its own citizens. Work relief is only a partial answer. Work and relief must pull in double harness through the thick gumbo of depression.

A final problem is the form that welfare organization should take. The poor-master and the politically organized department of welfare have become as outmoded as the stagecoach and the one-horse shay. Public welfare has become one of the most important departments in government. If we don't demand up-to-date vehicles for public welfare, as Arthur Dunham has pointed out, we shall either turn back to an outmoded system the great load left from the depression or maintain competing units of government.

Three things are highly important in this revamping of our welfare machine. There should be boards of highly qualified citizens appointed to give direction and to gear in public opinion. The one-man department partakes too much of dictatorship. Definite qualifications for personnel should be set up in order to insure the type of civil servants that the difficult problems of human beings demand. There should also be some form of state leadership of supervision since experience in the American form of government seems to have demonstrated that a better type of public service is secured under such conditions.

Recent Studies

The Federal Emergency Relief Administration, in its study of people on relief in the major cities, found that more than 80 per cent of the urban families on relief have at least one member who is able to work. The families without a breadwinner present a variety of circumstances, including families in which all the members are too young or too old to work, the physically handicapped, and women with small children.

This study with two other recent national ones are illuminating, especially when brought into relation with each other.

The second of these, by the Brookings Institution, *America's Ca-*

pacity to Consume, presents a carefully documented picture of American income and consumption. In 1929 there were 22 million non-farm families in the United States, 6 million farm families, and 9 million single individuals living by themselves. Of the city families, 7.5 million were on a poverty or a bare subsistence basis with a family income under $1,500; 7 million were on a minimum-comfort level with an income between $1,500 and $2,500; 7 million had over $2,500 per family per year.

Dr. Mordecai Ezekiel, the economic adviser to the Secretary of Agriculture, predicts what would happen if all the families were brought up to the $2,500 level. For the lowest income groups expenditures for education would be multiplied ten times, recreation five times, and medical care three times. There would be marked increases for food, housing, and clothing. The impetus of these increased expenditures upon the production of goods and the reduction in unemployment would be phenomenal.

Whether it is possible to bring this about is the immediate question, isn't it? But the third national study gives an answer in its two definite conclusions: "poverty prevails in the United States, and always has, but it need not exist in the future"; "an economy of abundance would result if production were directed toward the satisfaction of human needs and reasonable wants and restrained only by physical factors and the state of our knowledge."

This study also has revealed a marked shortage in the foodstuffs needed to provide an adequate diet. For instance, there is a deficiency of 2 billion pounds of butter, nearly 16 billion pounds of fruit, 77 billion pounds of whole milk—a sharp negation of the theory that we have too much and should therefore dump oranges into the sea. The survey also showed seriously low housing standards, insufficient clothing, growing obsolescence of machinery, and menacing deterioration in educational and health services.

Certain conclusions seem indicated from these studies. The large majority of those on relief can work and want work. Even before the depression years, over a third of the urban families in the United States were existing on a near-starvation level. The problem of unemployment and relief therefore is not emergent but constant—and one pressing for solution. Even with our great capacity to produce goods there has existed a serious shortage. The mere fulfilling of reasonable and human wants and desires would go a long way to put the wheels of industry whirring once more. There could be an economy of abundance and not of scarcity for the great mass of citizens if we had the vision and leadership to bring it to pass.

Further, we shall need some form of unemployment insurance, suited to the American pattern, in order to distribute better the hazards of unemployment. But as Paul H. Douglas of the University of Chicago estimates, even should Congress speed up the passage of such legislation actual payments could hardly begin before 1936 so we must face the fact that unemployment insurance will not ease the present situation. In other words, even though insurance becomes a part of the American economy, there will still remain need for a substantial relief program in future periods of deep unemployment. As Professor Douglas indicates: "the great merit of insurance is that it does not compel people to use up their individual savings and become virtually destitute before they can receive protection." Insurance is a cushion, not a permanent driving-seat.

Finally, like a peat fire eating underground, is the growing determination of masses of people that somehow social security must be provided for human beings. Nothing less will do. I recall the grim cartoon of the gnarled fist thrust up through the floor of a resplendent ballroom. That is a portent. The cry for bread by millions of our fellows is a negation of all that a Christian social order implies. We must dedicate ourselves to the task of helping to bring about an ordered world in which there shall be a decent way of life for all people. That is the enlarged task which social work has before it.

✔ **3. Some Chicago WPA workers.** In order to stop the "moral erosion" among unemployed people long on direct relief, the New Dealers in 1935 obtained legislation from Congress establishing the Works Progress Administration. The WPA differed from the earlier CWA (Civil Works Administration) in that it lasted for several years and undertook more substantial projects. On the other hand, its primary purpose was to provide work at minimal wages to people who would otherwise be on relief, and it could use only a small amount of its budget for tools and materials, unlike the PWA (Public Works Administration), which poured funds into construction materials and paid workers the prevailing wages. Between 1935 and 1941 it employed an average of 2,100,-000 workers on a wide variety of projects, paying them "security level" wages—less than regular employment and more than relief payments. The undertakings and experience of WPA workers were of an infinite variety; the attitudes of some of them are typified by these Chicagoans whom Margaret C. Bristol interviewed in the summer of 1936. *Margaret C. Bristol, "Personal Reactions* *of Assignees to WPA in Chicago,"* Social Service Review (*March 1938*), *84-87, 94, 95. Reprinted by permission of The University of Chicago Press.*

No. 19.—Mr. Bright is thirty-two years old and has a wife and nine children. He completed high school and then took a business course. Before applying for relief he spent fourteen years in various forms of auto mechanic work. He averaged about $20 a week. In 1933 the work became so scarce that he applied for public assistance. He received relief intermittently as he secured work for short periods. During the latter part of 1934 he was given work relief, first as a laborer and then as a timekeeper, and earned about $40 a month. He was not assigned to CWA but in November 1935 he received an assignment to WPA, as a timekeeper at a monthly wage of $85. He did this until February 1936, when he was transferred to another project and is now working as a truck-driver, delivering surplus commodities to relief families, still earning $85 a month. According to his statement pay checks are late, but he does not think that this can be helped for he has been a timekeeper and knows the difficulties. He finds it difficult to maintain his family on the amount earned for they do not receive supplementary assistance. He says that he is earning more now than he could anywhere else and because of this is not trying to locate other work. He does not believe that politics enters into the WPA situation at all for he has tried to exert pressure to get a better job but failed. He considers the work well operated and useful and says that all the men work hard and that most of the men who work need the jobs.

No. 20.—Mr. Panek was born in Czechoslovakia and came to this country in 1923 and is now fifty-two years of age. Four weeks prior to the interview, his wife died, leaving two children, a boy of seventeen and a girl of fourteen. Before the depression Mr. Panek earned $60 a week as a union cement-worker. In 1932, after several months of unemployment, he applied for relief at the public agency and in a short time was assigned to work relief as a laborer. He also was assigned to CWA but does not remember his wage. When this terminated he was again assigned to work relief but this time as a cement-finisher. His pay covered his entire budget of $60 a month. In November 1935, he was assigned to WPA and worked until March 1936 as a cement-finisher at $94 a month. At this time he received a nonrelief PWA job at $14 a day. Mr. Panek was quite enthusiastic about WPA and said that the work was well executed and of value to the community. However, he also stated that he realized that his particular work and the higher pay received would cause him to see conditions more favorably than if he had been earning $55 a month.

No. 21.—Mr. Mason is fifty-one years old and has his wife and sixteen-year-old son to support. Since 1912 he has been in the tire-repair and vulcanizing business. He has earned as much as $55 a week. Before he applied for relief in 1931 he had never had a shovel in his hand. He had lived on savings and on loans for two years before application for relief, and he still owes $500 and his rent is two years in arrears. He did not have a CWA job but was on work relief as a laborer for two years and then worked as a watchman and crossing guard. He contracted pleurisy on his last job and had to go back on direct relief for a while. He had received a work-relief rating on his physical examination of "C," owing to a weak heart and a dislocated spine which requires him to wear a truss. In November 1935, he went to work for WPA as a laborer at $55 a month. When he told his foreman that he could not do heavy work he was set to work painting the bleachers in Soldiers Field. He believes that politics is all mixed up with the administration of WPA and that "if you know the right kind of people you can get a better job." According to Mr. Mason their foreman is present every day but he is also drunk every day and uses vile language to the men, so it must be "pull that got him in and keeps him in." Mr. Mason prefers his WPA work to his work relief for he considers the work done on WPA to be more useful. He was embarrassed by his job as a crossing guard and did not think that type of work was necessary. There are always plenty of tools and materials on the WPA jobs. There are union men working on the same project who earn $13 a day while the other WPA men earn only $4 a day for the same work and this is very hard for the others. He says that the union men "lord" it over the rest.

No. 22.—Mr. Packard is a steam-hoist operator and at regular work earned about $70 a week. He was assigned as a laborer on work relief and earned his budget of $35 a month. He is now on WPA as a steam-hoist operator and earns $96 a month. In spite of the wage, the red tape, and the partisanship shown on the job, and the lateness of the checks cause him to dislike WPA. According to Mr. Packard the supervision is satisfactory. There are sufficient tools but they are often locked up until long after the men are supposed to start working. He believes that if a private contractor had the present job it would go twice as fast.

No. 24.—Mr. Wheeling is forty-eight years old and has a wife and six children, the oldest being a son of twenty-six years. He is a varnisher by trade earning $35 a week on the average. He lost his job in July 1930 and applied for assistance six months later. His work relief consisted of house painting and labor work at which he earned about $40 a month. He secured a private job for several months and when he had to return for relief he was assigned to a WPA job as a grader on a recreation field project. He earns $55 a month. He can see "no d—— sense in the project" and "the $150,000 being spent on the field house is a waste of money." According to Mr. Wheeling the men on the job do not work and so it may be at least two years before the job is finished. The men will not work because they are not being paid enough. He does not believe that any of the men are placed correctly —that none of the men were placed at their own trade. This, in Mr. Wheeling's estimation, confirmed his claim that the whole project was crooked and that the "higher-ups" were getting most of the money instead of allowing the men to receive a higher wage. He had gone to the Democratic ward committeeman for assistance in getting a better-paid job but this was not successful.

No. 25.—Mr. Robinson, who is fifty-six years old, and two children are supported by Mr. Robinson's WPA wages of $55 a month. One son is at a CCC camp and another hopes to go at the next registration. Mr. Robinson has been a truck-driver and at one time belonged to the union. He earned about $20 a week at this. The family applied for assistance in 1931, and in 1933 he was given his first work relief. For two months he worked on CWA at $24 a week. While on work relief he earned his budget part of the time and the rest of the time he earned very much less than this. A mistake was made for several months, and the family received almost $25 a month less than their budget. The mistake was not corrected until a doctor came in because of illness and found that they were suffering from malnutrition. During this time two of the boys suffered with heart trouble and were in the hospital part of the time. He worked on his first WPA job from November 1935 until April 1936 as a laborer at $55 a month and then was not reassigned until July 1936. He is now earning $55 as a laborer. He believes that the supervision on both projects was "pretty good" although some of the bosses knew their work and some did not. He does not believe that any of the men worked as hard on WPA as on a private job, but there have been plenty of tools and materials. Politics has never been discussed by the men but he thinks that the "dago" foremen get their jobs through "pull" or else "how would they get there." If he were offered a private job at the same money and under the same working conditions he would probably not accept it because the private job might not last. If the private job paid more money he would take it.

No. 39.—Mr. Krause is just twenty-three years old and his mother is dependent upon him as his father died fifteen years ago. He graduated from high school, where he had taken a science course together with aviation mechanics, but he has always done clerical work, earning $15 a week until he and his mother had to apply for assistance in 1932. He did not have CWA work but worked irregularly on work relief. He was at a CCC camp for six months and liked it very much and would like to return, but the $25 a month which he earned in camp is insufficient for his mother to live on, and they find that the two of them can live more comfortably on the $55 which he earns on WPA. For the first ten months he did street-repair work and then was transferred to a gardening project in Lincoln Park. This latter job is preferable to the first for he believes it to be more useful and necessary. According to Mr. Krause, WPA work has helped his morale, for he was "pretty discouraged when WPA came along and steady work has helped me to be self-respecting once again."

No. 42.—Mr. Dakin is forty years old and has a wife and three children under fourteen years of age. He is a decorator by trade and has done his own contracting. Mr. Dakin applied for assistance in 1931 and a year later was assigned to work relief where he earned $47 a month as a painter. Later he was assigned to WPA as a painter and is now earning $85 a month. Mr. Dakin is working on a school project which he considers useful, and in addition to the usefulness of the project he enjoys it because he is working at his regular trade. According to Mr. Dakin, the WPA work is better organized and more efficient and the projects are more useful than were those on work relief or CWA. He likes his work for he considers that payment for the work he has done is much more self-respecting than accepting direct relief.

✔ **4. A young man in the Civilian Conservation Corps.** The most popular of the relief agencies was the Civilian Conservation Corps which, in later years when other New Deal agencies were sharply criticized, continued to receive praise in the Republican press. At its height it enrolled about a half-million young men, who worked primarily at reforestation and flood control. This was no more than a fraction of the unemployed youth; some others received aid from the National Youth Administration. Stanley Watson, who later attended Washington State University, was one of many CCC workers who wrote accounts of their experiences. *A. C. Oliver, Jr., and H. M. Dudley, eds., This New Amer-*

ica, The Spirit of the Civilian Conservation Corps (*New York:
Longmans, Green and Co., 1937*), *pp. 3-8. Reprinted by permission of David McKay Company, Inc.*

Early in the winter of 1933 a ragged, shabby youth might have
been seen trudging Westward upon the national highway bearing the
number thirty. That youth was the writer of this article.

Out of work, discouraged, forsaken by those whom I thought to
be my friends, and worst of all without a home or shelter to which
to turn, I gathered my few belongings together and turned tramp.
This was December 1933. Not knowing where I was going, I turned
Westward, trudging disconsolately along the highway through a damp,
cold snowstorm. Depending on passing motorists for rides, I pro-
gressed rapidly until I neared the great plains area. I was becoming
sick and weak; the few dollars that I had had were gone; I was tired
and hungry for the first time in my life.

Too proud to beg for my food, I continued on to North Platte,
Nebraska, where cold weather forced me to ask humbly for shelter.
I was provided with this in the way of a canvas cot at the city hall,
but no feather bed or beauty rest mattress in the most expensive of
hotels would have felt better to me than that strip of canvas stretched
between two laths.

Morning dawned clear but exceedingly cold; the thermometer registered thirty-eight degrees below zero. My vanity would not allow me
to ask for food after having been lodged for the night; so, weak from
hunger, I resumed my journey Westward, with Cheyenne, Wyoming
as my goal for night. The day grew steadily colder; the pangs of
hunger gnawed upon my weakened body; but still I trudged onward,
determined to reach my goal. Dusk and then darkness found me still
short of my destination. At last I could see the lights of the city from
a distance. My strength was failing rapidly; I tried to hurry but to
no avail; I could no longer force myself to do the things against which
nature rebelled.

At noon the next day I was gently awakened by a beautiful, dark-
haired nurse and an army physician who wanted to know if I didn't
care to have some beef broth or hot milk toast. I would rather have
slept than eaten, but the doctor seemed to think I had slept long
enough for the time being and insisted that I drink some broth. When
I had finished, I asked him where I was and how I happened to be
there. I was in the Station Hospital at Fort Warren, Wyoming. I
had been picked up on the road outside of Cheyenne, overcome by lack
of nourishment and over-exposure in the bitter cold. For two weeks

I was confined to my bed and another week was spent regaining my strength before I was allowed again to take to the road.

When I left Cheyenne, I rode for the first time in a box car. My experience of the past few weeks had taught me a lesson. My pride vanished; I begged for my food and when I could not get it, I stole from my fellow unfortunates just as they did. A week or ten days later, I was in Seattle where I stopped at the home of relatives to clean up before resuming my travels.

When I had rested and refreshed myself, I started out bumming, begging my food and lodging, and pillaging when begging did not achieve the end to my satisfaction. I traveled in all of our forty-eight states, and I was rapidly becoming hardened to the coarser things of life. I went unshaven and dirty. I became lazy. Why should I work when I could eat three times a day without the outlay of a single copper or an ounce of energy? I became a master of sob-stories.

After eighteen months of riding box cars, begging and robbing for my food, fighting, dodging policemen, and committing other forms of petty larceny, I arrived in the village of Woodridge, New York, where I called upon an aunt and uncle. They talked to me of an organization called the Civilian Conservation Corps in which I could earn $30 a month and my board and room; I was amazed. I had never heard of it but at their insistence I promised to enlist and try it for one enlistment period. At last I was to have a home and something constructive to do.

I was first stationed at Narrowsburg, New York, in the midst of the beautiful Catskill Mountains. There, on the twenty-third of July, 1934, I began a life of discipline and supervision. It was a strange new life, but being a good mixer and having had the discipline of the road, I soon took hold.

The work of Company 1245 was divided into four phases, namely, the building of fire lanes, clearing and burning of brush, blister rust control and army overhead work. It was in the latter group that it fell my lot to work. My first assignment was that of a "galley slave," kitchen scully or K.P., call it what you may; I peeled vegetables, washed dishes, and scrubbed floors until I almost did them in my sleep.

I did my daily work diligently and precisely, working always for the one thing that was uppermost in my mind—advancement. I was working with a tall, dark-complexioned fellow who afterward was to become my most devoted friend. Two cousins of mine also worked with me. I wanted to gain a cook's position; so I spent a good share of my spare time around the ranges helping the cooks whenever possible.

Weekends when there was no work, those of us who were close enough went home. I spent my weekends with my aunt and uncle. During these periods of relaxation from the routine work of camp we had parties, went to dances, and engaged in many other forms of recreational activity. All too soon came the exciting yet disappointing message that we were to move to California. The trip across the continent was, for me, very dull and uneventful as I had roamed around over this same country not six months before. We arrived in Virgilio, California on the twenty-eighth day of October and walked into a camp location that made us all wonder why we had ever left good old New York. We were resigned to our fate, however; and within a few weeks, with hard work, had our camp in a very presentable condition.

As the months passed, new fellows came and the old went. With each coming and going, friendships were made and broken, new personalities appeared and new problems for those in charge. I recall one instance when a group of seven illiterates arrived in camp. The educational advisor, a young fellow just out of a well-known Midwestern school, threw up his hands in disgust. What could he do about it? He wasn't there to teach the alphabet; he had more important things to do. As a result these poor unfortunates went untutored. Those of us who had some education were given opportunity to advance ourselves. I studied sociology and sex hygiene—two very interesting and important subjects.

More recruits were coming into camp, and with each new group, the company's intelligence quotient dropped several points. The educational advisor (we had a new one) was very much disturbed but did little to remedy the fact. By January 1935 there were no less than fifteen illiterates in camp and had the educational record of the camp been published, it would probably read something like this: 7 per cent illiterate, 25 per cent with fourth-grade records, 40 per cent with eighth-grade diplomas, 30 per cent had entered high school but did not finish, and 3 per cent had high school diplomas. Not a very imposing tabulation for a group of 200, but nevertheless true.

March came and with it the end of an enlistment period. My dark-complexioned friend was going home; I tried to talk him into staying but he begged me to go home with him. Neither of us could see his way clear to accommodate the other. With our tears of parting mingled with those of others, we split the trail. March was an eventful month for me. I lost the only real pal and friend I had in camp; I achieved my ambition and was rated a first cook, but best of all, the camp got an educational advisor with plenty of vim, vigor, and vitality.

He stamped so strong an impression on me that I shall never forget him. He was short, fat, very jovial, and extremely well educated.

He received his Bachelor of Science and Master of Science degrees from Washington State College; and above all he had an active interest in his work. He not only saw the deplorable situation in our camp but took steps to overcome them. He selected three of us who he knew had high school diplomas and made us his helpers. He then divided the group of illiterates equally among us and told us to get to work. We did and thought the work was interesting from a psychological standpoint, but it was slow and tedious. After six months of constant teaching, all of the fifteen fellows were reading and writing.

A class in Poultry Husbandry was organized which I attended with intense interest. The educational advisor took a real liking to me and it was through his ever-ready tutoring and constant insistence that a new ambition was born within me. I decided to further my education, to go on to college. I worked diligently and saved my pay checks. Soon after deciding to go to college, I gained another promotion; I was made mess steward. In this capacity I gained experience that was to stand me in good stead later.

Evenings I took advantage of the many educational advantages offered to the enrollees. I studied Psychology, Sociology, and Speech. Through the winter I worked with but one picture in my mind—that of a beautiful green campus with big brick buildings and of myself going to and from classes—a beautiful picture if only it could be realized.

Spring came and summer. With each passing day, I looked forward with renewed eagerness to the day when I should say "Adieu" to my friends and again carry a textbook under my arm. Knowing that I would have to work my way through, I made several applications for work and received many offers, two of which I answered and accepted. Both were for cooks. Thank Heaven I had applied myself in this line for the duration of my enlistment. The knowledge I had acquired in the planning and preparation of meals was now to be a benefit.

On September the ninth I arrived in Pullman, Washington, to begin my duties; on the eighteenth I was enrolled and registered as a member in full standing in the freshman class. At the present time I am doing on the average of twenty-five hours work a week and am carrying a full schedule of school work. While I am not an outstanding student, I am managing to keep afloat and in pace with the average students of my class. My dreams have been realized, thanks to an educational advisor and the lessons learned in the CCC.

The Great Drive Toward Recovery

✓ **5. Sherwood Anderson reports the mood of small-town workers.** "The law I have just signed," proclaimed President Roosevelt as the National Recovery Administration was about to come into being, "was passed *to put people back to work,* to let them buy more of the products of farm and factories and start out business at a living rate again." Section 7-a of the Act, which provided that "employees should have the right to organize and bargain collectively," gave a sharp stimulus to union activities. Nevertheless by the winter of 1933-34 it was all too apparent that the NRA was falling far short of early expectations. Sherwood Anderson, famous as the author of *Winesburg, Ohio,* traveling on a roving assignment for Raymond Moley, editor of *Today,* found many workers still unemployed, some of them perhaps permanently so. What they wanted was not relief but jobs and security in their jobs, and they pinned their hopes on the New Deal recovery program. *Sherwood Anderson, "I Want to Work!" Today (April 28, 1934), 10-11, 22. Reprinted by permission of Newsweek, Inc. The original source* Today *is now defunct.*

Recovery—rapid recovery within a matter of months—was the first great positive objective of the New Deal. Americans greeted with enthusiasm the two major recovery measures passed in the spring of 1933, the Agricultural Adjustment Act to raise the income of farmers, and the National Industrial Recovery Act. Currency devaluation to counter the severe deflation of previous years was a third important facet of the recovery program, but most people focussed their attention upon the AAA and the NRA.

The continuous talking with men and women, going into houses, into churches, union halls, meeting men on the street, getting into talk with them. . . . "Have a cigaret." . . . "Come on, let's go eat, have a glass of beer" . . . this coming of beer helps. . . .

Preachers in small town and city churches . . . doctors . . . some of whom have been mill town doctors; young doctors often get a start that way; some of them get out into general practice but hang on to friends made among the workers. In some of the churches and Sunday schools they begin to discuss the advisability or inadvisability of workers joining unions.

The New Deal has cracked something open. In the South and pretty much all over the United States there was, before Roosevelt came, a feeling that to have anything to do with a union meant a certain social blight. "Not me. I do not intend to stay down here. I'm going to rise in the world." The taint on labor, particularly in the South, is an old thing. It probably has its roots in chattel slavery. A gentleman or a gentlewoman didn't soil his or her hands.

President Roosevelt has, by recognition of the possible value of labor organizations, torn open a door.

"Is labor rising effectually to its opportunity?"

"No," they say. The workers growl. Professional men in the towns, country lawyers—in pretty close touch—laugh. They say: "If labor doesn't come into new power now, find broad-minded effective leadership, it isn't the President's fault."

The leaders of public opinion in the towns . . . small town lawyers . . . the crowd from which, in the past, have come most of our American political leaders, scoff at the professors, the so-called "Brains

Trust." The scorn isn't very deep-seated. It's easy to put such a one on the defensive. "Did you admire Woodrow Wilson?" "Yes, I did. He was a great man, had a great dream."

"Say, why did you go to college? Why do you send your son and daughter to school?

"It's a bit odd, isn't it . . . we Americans have been so hot on education . . . we all want it for our sons and daughters . . . then, when some man gets it. . . .

"Oh, I didn't mean it. I was just joshing you."

In reality, half of it is resistance to change, any kind of change. The President's job isn't just to get people back to work, get higher prices for farm products. There is a bigger job he has already begun, a kind of striking down into men's imaginations. It has already gone pretty far.

I went to a meeting of negro workers. Even the illiterate ones can listen to the radio. Just because a man can't read or write doesn't necessarily mean that he hasn't a mind. I have found that out myself, living these last five years among mountain men in southwest Virginia. I have tried trading horses with some of my neighbors who cannot read or write. . . .

The negroes were at their meeting discussing the same things I had heard discussed in a Sunday school class . . . labor, the yellow dog contract, the lockout, advisability of labor getting itself intelligently organized. . . . "If a man like President Roosevelt thinks labor should organize, why shouldn't I think so?" That is the notion.

At the meeting of negroes a black man got up and proposed that, at the next meeting to be held, he bring his preacher.

There were objections, apologetic but determined objections. "I believe in God and His son, Jesus Christ, but there is the carnal and the uncarnal. We have come here to talk about the carnal. We have to talk among ourselves."

In a speech somewhere Secretary Wallace said: ". . . I don't belong to the personal devil school of economics." I didn't hear the speech. A Southern country town lawyer told me about it. I had been to a meeting of a town social club on the evening before and we had walked out together. He escorted me back to my hotel.

There is a mistake constantly being made by our professional radicals. It concerns this very matter of personal devils. Time and again I have seen it. There is a strike at some mill and often some speaker who begins a bitter personal attack upon the mill owner or manager. I have heard a good many such speeches and have watched the audience. It doesn't work, doesn't go over. As though voices were calling up out of the audience: "That isn't it. That isn't the point. Keep to the point." On the way out of such a meeting I hear one striker speaking to another. "I don't know," he says. "I don't know how hard-boiled I'd be if I got on top once."

It would be curious if the President could shift this belief in the rights of the individual to rise, say, above his fellows, get wealth and power, to some real acceptance of individual responsibility, as though to say, "it would be more fun, would get me further." A worker said to me, "There's Mr. Roosevelt . . . it's funny . . . I never heard anyone say whether he has money of his own or not. They tell me how rich some of the movie actors are, some of the Senators, the bankers, etc. They say money means power. I guess if he was very rich they'd tell about it. I don't know any man in American history who has had more power."

As though to say again . . . "evidently there's another kind of power to be got."

You will see that I am trying to hint at something picked up in my wanderings this Winter . . . doors to the minds and imaginations of ordinary men a little opened. I have heard amazingly little whining. You simply cannot do what I have been doing without getting some feeling of admiration for the Americans who, in the last few years, have been getting it in the neck.

Minds everywhere centered upon the job. It is the American passion.

"I want to work, feel myself a part of things."

It is true I know that you cannot build too much on individual cases. Often I go about for hours, in industrial towns, seeing people, men and women, out-of-works, factory hands hurrying to or from factories, men and women at gatherings, union meetings, meetings of the unemployed . . . wanting to stop every man and woman met . . . farmers . . . "Tell me your story. What do you feel?"

There is the big shapeless mass. You want to pry into it. You can't very deeply, not in a few weeks or months, perhaps not in a lifetime. . . .

I have talked to many manufacturers, factory superintendents, and rarely, I think never, have I gone into a shop without being shown some new machine.

Here, in a tin can factory, is a machine that makes can tops. It is the superintendent of the shop showing me through. "When I first came to work here, when I first became a foreman, we had a machine that turned out forty can tops a minute. There was a man at work on every machine. Now you see this long battery of machines. The two men you see walking up and down take care of them all. They don't work so hard. There isn't any heavy work in any modern shop.

"When I was a young man here, a young foreman, I used to go home at night, having seen a new machine installed that would knock out forty can tops a minute. I used to think: 'Are there people enough in the world to use so many tin cans?'" He laughed. "Look at these machines," he said, with pride in his voice. "Every machine, in this long row of machines is knocking out 360 can tops a minute."

"And you have laid off many men who can never get back into this shop?"

"Yes."

"I do not see many older men."

"No. The younger ones have the call. They are quicker, you see, less likely to get hurt."

I asked him what I have asked many men in positions of control in industry. "When you are all doing it, laying off so many men who can never get back, aren't you laying off your own customers, users of the goods you make here?"

"Yes, we are, all right."

"Well, what are you fellows going to do?"

"I don't know."

That attitude on the part of most of the men in control of the shops. What about the workmen?

Those who say that American workmen, so often now thrown out of their place in our social and economic scheme by the modern machine, so often robbed of something peculiarly vital to their feeling of manhood . . . this I keep thinking the most important thing of all, the thing I keep hoping that Washington may come more and more to understand and appreciate. . . .

The machines themselves apparently becoming always faster and faster, more and more efficient with the coming of NRA . . . the man in the street can see it with his own eyes in the increased beauty, speed and efficiency of the automobile. . . .

As though there were actually a kind of devil sleeping down in these so-gorgeously beautiful masses of steel in action. . . .

Those who hold that American workmen do not want to work with the machines, that they do not want to be in the factories, simply do not know what they are talking about.

In the greater majority of American workmen, and now in American workwomen, actual love of the machines and . . . yes, I am sure of it . . . in spite of everything . . . love of the factories. There are, to be sure, always the stupid ones, the dull ones, but the numbers of the other constantly amazes.

The workman, past his prime, who knew what had happened to him and with whom I drank the beer, had got into the habit of going into the public library of the town. As I have said, we were in a Southern town. "I was born a Yank," he said.

"So was I," I said.

His father, a carriage blacksmith, had come South after the war, when he was a young boy.

"The kids here used to dog me a lot about being a Yank.

"So I thought, sometime, I thought, when I have time, I'm going to read up on that war.

"I'd never been much to read."

He had got on to one of my own hobbies. "Well," I said.

"Now there was Grant," he said. "I've got to liking that man, at least to liking what he was when he was just a general, before he got to be President. He wasn't such a smart man, but I figure he had a big idea all right."

"Yes? And how?"

"I been figuring it out. I've got plenty of time to figure things out. A lot of the Northern generals during the war couldn't see the war as a whole. That's what made it last so long."

"You mean?"

"You see, I figure, they thought of a battle as a battle. I think he saw the war as a war."

"He and Lincoln, eh?"

"Yes," he said.

"I've been thinking," he said, "that this Roosevelt, maybe . . .

"He may see it as a whole, what we are up against.

"Not just me," he said, "I mean all of us. North and South now."

"You mean the factory owners, those who are in work and those who are out. . . .

"And the farmers, too?"

"Yes, and the dead ones like me," he said quickly, "the ones they can't use any more.

"I've been thinking," he said, "from what I've read and what I've heard him say that he gets the picture."

I left him sitting in the room and went down the stairs and into the street and on the next day I got into the factory where he had been employed. It was a good one, very modern, very big, light and efficient.

On the day when I left him and got into the street I wasn't thinking of that.

"They are O.K. They can sure take it," was what I was thinking.

✔ **6. NRA: A trial balance.** At the end of May 1935, when the Supreme Court invalidated the code system of the National Recovery Administration, there was both jubilation and apprehension throughout the country. Few were entirely agreed as to what the NRA had meant to the American people or what had been its measure of success and failure. The head of the Textile Division of the NRA, M. D. Vincent, a notable Colorado lawyer and reformer, with the aid of a *Survey Graphic* staff writer, prepared an incisive estimate of the effect of the codes. *M. D. Vincent and Beulah Amidon, "NRA: A Trial Balance,"* Survey Graphic (*July 1935*), *333-37, 363-64. Reprinted by permission of Helen Hall.*

The Supreme Court decision in the Schechter case has brought to an abrupt end our first experiment in exercising a measure of public control over the industrial life of the country. Then ten months ahead, with a "stop-gap" NRA, will be a time to assay the work of the past two years and also to observe, with competition free except for the anti-trust laws, what standards of wages, hours and fair trade practices industry sets for itself. It is obviously impossible at this date to make any final summary of the brief NRA experience. Further, the Brookings Institution study has already demonstrated that evaluation of NRA as a recovery instrument depends wholly on the definition of "recovery" with which one starts. This article will not attempt to prove that NRA either succeeded or failed. Drawing on the experience as a division administrator of one of the writers and on such data as is now available in Washington, it will attempt some answers, although frankly incomplete, to the question, What happened under the codes?

It is necessary to keep in mind the pre-code picture. Following the 1929 crash, the drop in wage payrolls soon reached $9 billion and within three years farm crop values shrank 60 per cent. There was a tailspin and crash in the prices of merchandise commonly used in the greatest volume. There was a rapid rise in the number of unemployed from 3 million, which appalled us, to 13 or 14 million. The nation was precipitated into the state of complete confusion that culminated in the national bank holiday, in March 1933.

President Hoover's White House conference of business leaders in November 1929 disagreed on everything except that there must be no lowering of purchasing power, hence no wage cuts. The reaction to this was the famous dictum of the banker, Albert Wiggin: "Money has taken its wage cut, and so must labor." Wage and work standards crumbled. This "voluntary agreement" proved futile to safeguard

wage-earners, home markets or business. Industry continued the peril-
ous downward spiral, until the new administration came in, when the
NIRA was enacted. The purpose of the Act, as stated in its preamble,
was to check the drop in purchasing power and production and the
rise in business mortality; to substitute for unregulated competition,
"cooperative action among trade groups" and "united action of labor
and management under adequate governmental sanctions and supervision."

It was proposed to accomplish these objectives by shortening hours
of work, setting minimum-wage levels, establishing fair trade standards as checks to destructive competitive practices, relaxing the anti-
trust laws and safeguarding labor's right to organize. Agreements to
this end were expected to flow from the united action of labor and
management, "in partnership with government" acting through the
National Recovery Administration.

The codes of fair competition were designed to implement these
plans. There were no rules and no precedents for code-making, no
guides except the very general provisions of the Act, no definition of
policy or of standards. The final form in which a code emerged was
the joint product of the deputy administrator presiding at the hearings
and his advisers, and of representatives of industry and labor facing
him with their diverse demands. Most codes provided for a minimum-wage rate, a maximum hours standard, a limited apprentice or
beginner tolerance, the elimination of child labor. The collective bargaining provision of the Act (Section 7-a) was written into each code
by law. Beyond that there was wide diversity in provisions for limitation of machine hours, trade practices, and in those provisions designed
to fix or influence prices. There were no uniform and definite standards of cost accounting or assembly of basic industrial data. In other
words, the codes represented a process, not a planned product.

Though they were held to be codes by mutual agreement or assent,
the assent by both management and labor was often reluctantly given.
It is, we believe, quite accurate to say that the assent or agreement
was rather acquiescence under fear of the consequences of failure to
agree. On February 1, 1935, there were 546 codes, covering more
than 2½ million firms and some 22 million workers. In the Textile
Division, on the experience of which this article will draw heavily,
there were 97 codes, covering 41,000 firms with 2¼ million workers.

Through the code authorities, industry was given broad opportunity
to demonstrate its capacity for self-discipline and self-government
under the official supervision of NRA. In its last (though no one
viewed it as final) form, NRA was made up of the National In-

dustrial Recovery Board, division administrators and their staffs of deputies and assistant deputies, a research and planning division, legal division, compliance division, and industry, labor and consumer advisory boards. For administrative purposes, industries were grouped in twelve divisions, with a division administrator at the head of each. Deputy administrators with their staffs had immediate administrative charge of the codes.

Confronted with the question: "What did the codes accomplish and what did they fail to accomplish?" final conclusions must be avoided. Certain developments, trends and effects are obvious. Others are as variable as the conditions out of which they flow. But though appraisal of total results is not possible at this time, we can point to some definite effects of code provisions on business operations and on the lives of those touched by them, both as workers and as consumers. At the same time, it is necessary to bear in mind that many influences in addition to NRA were at work.

Let us look first at the provisions most directly affecting workers in the coded industries: those regulating wages, hours, child labor, industrial homework.

One of the most widely accepted code provisions was the one prohibiting child labor. Though newsboys were not covered, nearly 125,000 children under sixteen were taken out of the labor market, their jobs in factories, mines, shops, offices made available to unemployed adults. Unfortunately, few developments under the codes were so direct, so definite, and so unanimously approved.

Code regulation of hours and wages had a three-fold purpose: to increase employment by reducing the workday or the workweek; to protect living standards; to build up domestic markets for farm products and manufactured goods. . . .

Two studies of the same plants, the first made in February 1934, the second in February 1935, showed an 11 per cent increase in employment, a rise in payrolls from $7,600,000 to $10,200,000; an increase in average hourly earnings from 36.6 cents to 42.3 cents ($11.78 weekly to $13.07 weekly) ; a drop in average man-hours per week from 32.2 to 30.9.

In a statistical report on the first eighteen months of NRA, dated January 1, 1935, the Research and Planning Division found that in coded industries wage rates had increased 30 per cent, in non-code industries, 10 per cent, adding, "This should not be taken to mean that the effect of the codes is 20 per cent." The biggest increases were found in industries where rates were lowest. In industries where rates were already high (machines, machine tool, printing, for example) the rise was small. . . . The Research and Planning report concludes:

> There have been increases in wage rates nothing short of phenomenal wherever the previous rate was low, that is for labor working in low-paid industries, for labor living in the South, particularly female labor, for labor living in towns of less than 20,000 population, for labor in low-paid occupations, in a word, for labor getting very low pay anywhere coming under the codes.

But figures cannot tell the whole story. There are thousands of letters in NRA files—laboriously pencilled notes, many of them—which put in more vivid terms some of the things the charts and figures indicate. For instance, a woman in a Midwestern factory town wrote:

> The fair employer who wants to pay his workers a living wage is certainly for the NRA. The NRA places a minimum wage, so the man paying $13 a week don't have to compete with one paying $3 a week. Those who don't like the NRA never worked in a sweat-shop 80 hours a week and received $3.50 for pay such as I have right in ———— City or they would not take this attitude.

Sidney Hillman, head of the Amalgamated Clothing Workers of America and one of the most able members and accurate critics of NRA stated before the Senate Finance Committee:

> In my judgment minimum wages are too low—entirely too low—but we can show tens of thousands and hundreds of thousands of workers who were compelled to accept wages as low as 10 cents an hour, 5 cents an hour, 3 cents an hour, who have at least the protection of 24 cents an hour, 30 cents an hour, 40 cents an hour.

The cut in hours was also most striking in the low-paid groups. . . . But changes in the length of the average workweek were widespread. . . . On the questions of hours and employment, as well as wages, letters from workers are eloquent. Here is a paragraph from a letter from the Southwest:

> If the poor people could only express themselves like the rich there would be no question as to whether NRA had been a benefit to the working classes or not. Before NRA some of the girls in the factories here had to work as long as 12 hours a day for about $7 a week. Never before have the working-people here enjoyed their work as in the past two years under NRA.

A man in a large industrial city wrote:

> There are 20 of us making $15 a week and working 48 hours a week. But without the code all that would change in one day. There would

be 15 of us working and we would do 68 hours a week for $10 in each pay envelope. That was the way it was before a code.

A woman in another industry in the same city stated:

> Before the New Deal came into effect we was compelled to work 15 hours of each day during the rush and no overtime and fired if you get a [union] card. Now we got our union and we got our decent work-week and we got more girls working here and we got better wages. Where I used to never get more than $8 a week now I don't never get under $13.50. Our life is no bed of roses because that aint the way it is for the workers yet but it's better for us than ever I seen it and I been in a factory 9 years since I was 15.

A Southern mill-worker's letter reads, in part,

> I used to draw $6 for 9 days' work and very long hours. Now I draw $12.50 a week and no day over 8 hours. That is a big difference and our life is different and there is a chance for a happy home. But if there was no code I cannot bear to think how it will be once more.

Information compiled by the Research and Planning Division underscores the statement of many economists and labor groups, "Minimum wages are too low." . . . But the most ominous statistics of the recovery effort to date are to many persons those comparing corporate earnings and wages. A selected group of 639 corporations showed an increase in net earnings of 519 per cent between 1932 and 1934. For the same period, average weekly earnings in industries bracketing those corporations increased 5 per cent. Concerning this, another paragraph from the Research and Planning Division report should be kept in mind. Stating that between June 1933 and December 1934, the indices of the U.S. Bureau of Labor Statistics showed, a 20 per cent increase in production (63.9 to 78.2); a 16 per cent increase in employment (63.9 to 74.6); a $33\frac{1}{3}$ per cent increase in payrolls (43.2 to 57.9), the report adds:

> On the whole, the amount of money which the average workingman in industry under the codes finds in his pay envelope has not increased a great deal, the increases in payroll apparently going to added workers, formerly unemployed.

The increase in employment during the code period is variously estimated at from 2 to 3 million.

A number of factors operated to keep the workers from getting the full benefit even of such low wage minima as were set by the codes. In some instances, the minimum wage tended to become the maximum. More frequently wage increases in classifications above the minimum were defeated by various types of speed-up and stretch-out. In the men's clothing code, for example, there was a provision to maintain existing differentials in the higher-paid groups and to keep the minimum from becoming the "going rate" for the industry. There were also "equitable adjustment provisions" in other codes. A sample study of the men's clothing industry for the 1934 fall season was made by the Research and Planning Division. It covered 1472 establishments with 99,107 workers, and included the 50 largest units in the industry; over 650 smaller establishments, and about 700 contractors. Under the code, a minimum wage of 40 cents an hour (with geographic differentials) was established. In the 1934 fall season, the average wage for the industry was 66.2 cents an hour—$23.82 for a 36-hour week. The 1933 pre-code weekly average was slightly above $12. Employment in the industry had increased in the same period from 109,000 to 125,000. The study found that 19.7 per cent of the workers in the industry were receiving only the code minimum. But among individual employers the range was from less than 1 per cent of the employees to more than 80 per cent. Nearly 56 per cent of the workers in the industry were receiving 50 cents an hour or better, but here again there was a wide range as between employers. Some paid less than 7 per cent of their workers at this rate, others paid 50 cents an hour or more to 97 per cent. The study concluded that:

> For the most part a wage policy within the spirit and letter of NRA has been carried out by the overwhelming majority of larger manufacturers, smaller manufacturers and contractors, and . . . only a selfish few are for the most part paying only the minimum or slightly above the minimum.

It is nevertheless true that there are important and in some instances prosperous industries which do pay code rates but whose wage rates are too low. They are not returning to the market in the form of wages an amount equal to their ability to pay nor proportionately what other industries are paying. Such industries are obstructing the development of our potential markets.

The Textile Division of NRA included some admirable examples of well-organized industry and intelligent cooperation between management and labor. At the same time, it included most of the homework industries, which afford probably the most flagrant American examples of helpless, exploited workers. Homework, jobbed out by manufacturers or contractors to tenement or rural homes, means child labor in most lines and is the lowest paid of all labor. Its usual wage range is from a few cents to $5 a week. Of the 546 codes, 86 prohibited homework, 11 limited it, while 9 codes specifically continued homework with some sort of control.

In reporting on industrial homework under NRA in March 1935, the Pennsylvania State Labor Department found:

> The number of homeworkers reported by Pennsylvania employers decreased from 8,649 to 5,531 between September 1933 and September 1934, a drop of more than one-third. This decrease resulted mainly from the prohibition of homework by many NRA codes. . . . The code of fair competition for the men's clothing industry . . . set the precedent for complete prohibition . . . and 1,300 jobs were moved from homes to factories [in this state]. . . . As a result of the various code prohibitions, the homework problem is now concentrated in a comparatively small number of industries. . . .

Under NRA as under state regulation, homework remained a thorny problem. No satisfactory totals showing its extent, its hours and wages, night work, and child labor have ever been compiled, nor any method of collecting them devised. But it is fair to say that progress in dealing with the problem was being made as was shown by Pennsylvania's experience and by the Children's Bureau study, which concludes, in part:

> While there is no doubt that, in those industries in which the code prohibits homework, some "bootlegging" is going on and that unscrupulous manufacturers are still making use of the system in violation of their codes, it cannot be denied that the volume of homework has greatly decreased since the prohibitions went into effect. Investigators of the Department of Labor, while carrying on the present study, report that they experienced considerable difficulty in locating persons actually engaged in homework in sections where in past years had only to walk along certain streets to see entire families absorbed in work that is now abolished under the codes.

NRA established the Compliance Division to enforce labor and trade practice provisions. It was also a policy to authorize code authorities to set up their own committees to enforce labor and trade practice provisions. . . .

To May 27, 1935, the Compliance Division had made wage adjustments in 74,520 cases, with more than $6 million paid in restitution to workers.

What the functioning of the compliance machinery meant in such cases was eloquently expressed by a New England worker, who wrote:

> The most surprising day ever seen in this place was yesterday when the boss was ordered to pay us at the code rate and more than that was ordered to give us what was due at that rate from the be-

ginning of the code and we got the money right in our hands. You can guess that the money is handy. With the $41.80 coming to me we can do a lot. But there is something more than the money. There is knowing that the working man don't stand alone against the bosses and their smart lawyers and all their tricks. There is a government now that cares whether things is fair for us. I tell you that is more than money. It gives you a good feeling instead of all the time burning up because nothing is fair.

In establishing the right of labor to organize, less progress was made than in establishing and safeguarding standards of wages and hours. Labor accepted without reservation the full import of all sections of the Recovery Act. Large groups of employers refused to accept Section 7-a, the collective bargaining provision, and resisted its application. Labor resented this disregard of its rights under the law, and the conflict was the most bitter of those which arose under the codes. Management sought to interpret 7-a in ways which qualified its meaning. It is justifiable to say that every intelligent worker and every intelligent employer knows exactly what 7-a means. No question respecting its meaning has arisen where management and labor voluntarily accepted it. The difficulties arising under this section occurred only when management opposed the principle of collective bargaining and refused to make collective agreements. The stock challenge to 7-a was that it did not give representation to minority groups of workers. The answer is simple: it was not intended to let minority groups, dominated by the employer or acting independently, defeat the working terms and conditions which a majority might be able to negotiate. The provision was based on the democratic principle of representation. That system does not subject majorities to the control of minorities, either when applied to government or to private business transactions.

Many code authorities admitted their inability to enforce fair trade practices except a few universally accepted rules, which we may say are the equivalent of, "You shall not steal." No industrialist will publicly resist such regulations. Outside this clear and narrow field one gets into the realm of ethics where there are vast possibilities for misunderstanding and evasion. Concealed discounts, for example, are difficult, sometimes impossible to detect and are devastating in their consequences. But a rule against them cannot be enforced except in occasional instances, largely because many wholesalers, jobbers, manufacturers and retailers insist that such a discount is "fair competition." In many instances, as in volume buying, there is advantage to the manufacturer in reduced selling cost and more continuous operation, which is treated as a fair consideration for the concession.

In some highly organized industries with comparatively few members, most of whom have large investments, trade practice enforcement was successful. It is perhaps more accurate to say that in such situations compliance was voluntary. Where, however, an industry had numerous units distributed over wide areas, except for a few universally accepted standards, "fair practice" provisions did not stand up. This was especially true in manufacturing industries in which one could go into business on small capital. When a man is operating on a shoestring, he is not particularly sensible of an obligation to play a game in which the rules were written by those with more at stake. Nevertheless, there was sufficient enforcement or compliance to curb and in many lines to eliminate much of the destructive force of vicious market habits. On the basis of a two-year experiment it is impossible to say how much more could have been done with further opportunity for education within business and industry, for developing enlightened public opinion and for refining policy and procedure. Even this limited NRA experience forcibly suggests that the term "fair competition" is difficult to define. Not since the beginning of machine production has there been "fair competition" in the old, handcraft-era sense in making or merchandising any widely used commodity. Apparently the most constructive line of effort would be to define some of the factors of *unfair* competition and seek to ban such practices through the intelligent cooperation of producer, distributor, worker and consumer.

In order to save some situations, NRA had resort to arbitrary limitation of production. While the immediate effect of machine-hour limitation might be to check business failures, price slashing or layoffs, it inevitably reallocated business from the efficient to the inefficient producer. Perhaps such limitation may be regarded as a legitimate expedient in a time of adjustment, but there is danger in over-reliance upon it, and in the tendency to treat arbitrarily curtailed production as a remedy, disregarding the long-range economic desirability of wider production and distribution.

NRA has demonstrated that what we call legitimate competition is confined to the field of management in which any advantage in the market goes, as it should, to the most efficient. The destructive competition of which we have experienced so much uses labor costs as its chief instrument with which to undersell and take the competitors' business. This competition takes money out of labor's pocket and thereby ultimately removes much of it from trade channels by transferring it to idle surplus profits. In a profit system a bedrock price policy may produce a temporary increase of profits by an increase of sales volume, but it will not permanently support high wages or high profits and will eventually diminish sales volume and therefore artificially restrict production.

Freedom from anti-trust laws to fix prices provoked wide discussion and much criticism. A number of industries had approved code provisions authorizing cost systems as a basis for price fixing, to prevent selling below cost, and price-filing provisions. These were watched with questioning interest by NRA. It early became evident that it is impracticable if not impossible through government agencies to prevent excessive prices to safeguard the consumer. Office Memorandum No. 228, June 7, 1934, declared price fixing to be contrary to policy. Provision was made, however, for "price floors" in cases of emergency to prevent destructive price cutting. Long established price-cutting practices in an industry were not, however, treated as such an emergency. Consequently, emergency orders authorizing fixed minimum prices were rarely granted. Many industries did not, however, seek or resort to price fixing and do not want it.

There is no doubt that cost of living, that is, prices of consumer goods, advanced more rapidly than wages, although prices were more stable in code than in noncode industries. Many factors serve to modify "normal" price trends. "Price lines" are increasingly the rule in retail merchandising, such as standard prices for different types of dresses, shoes and other goods. Consumer demand is built upon such price lines, and manufacturers have to produce to them. Obviously, production costs are under the pressure of the retailer's demand for better and better quality of material and workmanship in an established price line in which competition is keen. The consumer's first interest should be not in the lowest price but in a fair price. The pressure of competition often obscures this fact, and also obscures the further fact that a break in wage and hour rates to meet competition adds to unemployment and contracts purchasing power. In this vicious circle the small manufacturer and his employees are more frequently the first victims, as he is often the first offender. Sidney Hillman told at the Senate Finance Committee hearings how the small manufacturer, unable to send out salesmen, must go to the chain distributor:

> . . . and what he does is really sell labor, and the pressure from these big people is always 'Get it cheaper.' Today is the first time he can tell them, 'We cannot get it cheaper, the government will not permit us to do it.' . . . And we must not lose sight of the fact that 5 per cent of the chiselers who have no conscience—and they have demonstrated during the depression they have no conscience and human values mean nothing to them—they start out underselling the rest of them, and the 95 per cent must follow or go out of business. . . . One big chain store starts selling a shirt for 27 cents and what

are the others to do? They must sell that shirt for 27 cents. . . .
How do they do it? Crush labor.

What the code protection meant to the small manufacturer and
business man is shown not only in . . . the Dun and Bradstreet
record of commercial failures over a period of years, but much more
eloquently in letters and telegrams in NRA files. There is space to
quote only two, but they are typical of hundreds. The first is a tele-
gram from the head of a small eastern plant:

> Our average weekly payroll February 1933 was $7,014 for 370
> employes. February 1935, $9,335 for 425 employes. Doesn't this say
> something coming from a medium small plant in a country village in
> behalf of the company and its wage-earners under the code?

The second is from a letter from a Western manufacturer, received in
April 1935:

> In my own plant I paid 25 per cent more wages for 1934 than I
> did for 1933 and more wages than I have paid since 1931. I also paid
> an income tax for 1934, the first since 1930.

In looking back over NRA experience, one fact is outstanding. The
controlling factor in the experiment was good management. The best
examples of progress under the codes were in well-organized industries, with active, established cooperation between management and
labor. Conversely, the areas in which NRA fell conspicuously short
of its goals corresponded very closely with the areas in which management and labor failed to cooperate. While large sections of industry
went along with NRA, and labor went along wholeheartedly, relations
between management and labor were not much, if at all, improved.
Perhaps the most regrettable shortcoming of NRA is the fact that
despite explicit provisions of the Act, industry in general did not
embrace the opportunity to establish rational and workable relations
with its employees.

How much of the gain under NRA can be preserved and continued
it is too early to say. Front-page statements by trade associations and
industrial leaders announce that code standards of hours and wages
will be continued. Less encouraging are the reports which labor
organizations and NRA offices, in these closing days, are receiving
from all sections of the country. As this is written, the American
Federation of Labor is releasing a report which begins:

> A special telegraphic survey . . . supplemented by reports from
> other organizations, reveals that at least a million wage earners

throughout the nation have been affected by the lengthening of hours of work and wage cutting in a short span of six business days following the Supreme Court decision.

The report includes a list of forty-three industries where "important violations of labor standards have taken place."

Letters from individuals, written under the strain of fear and uncertainty, sharpen this picture. From a widowed factory worker:

> Before the 40-hour week went into effect, I work from 8 in the morning until 8 at night. Now my children got used to having me at home. . . . How can I stand that terrible long, routine again?

This is from a Midwestern town:

> I am a salesman in a chain store. Before NRA I worked 7 A.M. to 10 or 11 P.M. Now two of us work 8 hours a day each. If they don't extend NRA one of us gets fired and the other works 14 or 15 hours.

Brief and to the point is this sentence from a petition signed by more than 100 workers in a small Atlantic-seaboard community: "Without NRA the undersigned would be out of jobs and our children back in the mill."

Along with reports of longer hours and lower wages are indications that cuts in wholesale and retail prices, many of which ignore costs, are spreading. The consumer who is likewise either the producer or the distributor cannot simultaneously enjoy high wages and bedrock prices. If he is to have healthy wage standards and working conditions he must under any economic system pay at least fair prices for the merchandise produced under such standards. Since the wholesale and retail distributor depends upon the consuming industrial and farm populations to maintain markets, as do the professional classes for their income, there is a community responsibility in which all these groups are included. An expanding production and distribution of farm and factory goods presupposes prices stabilized at levels which assure a constant even though gradual increase in wage, salary and farm income, and a sufficient margin of profit to insure a return on investment, or at least, on real values. Forty years' experience with the anti-trust laws has shown that their power to restrain is theoretical. In operation under judicial application they have done little more than express a hope. The freedom that these theoretical restraints have actually permitted is expressed in the business structures and economic influences which contributed in large measure to the conditions NRA was designed to correct.

If the release of business and industry by the Supreme Court decision from government control is but an open door of return to those practices which contributed to the demoralization of domestic markets and values, it cannot be expected that the victims will patiently submit to a continuing government policy of hands off. The public has felt for a brief time the effect of public control, even though in a most limited sense. It now knows that effective action under government leadership is possible. It believes that government has the inherent power to safeguard both public and private security. The uncertainty and bewilderment created by the Supreme Court's decision is very likely to be dispelled by an unyielding demand for permanent public regulation of those economic forces and agencies which private management is unable to organize and control.

✔ 7. **Money in the farmer's mailbox.** Through the Agricultural Adjustment Administration, producers of seven basic commodities received government aid in limiting production in order to obtain higher prices. These producers, through the "domestic allotment" plan, received benefit payments (raised through a tax on the processed commodities) in return for reducing acreage or production. The scheme was one which had been advocated by leaders of farm organizations representing the more successful farmers. Walter Davenport reported in *Colliers* how Middle Western farmers were reacting to the benefit payments they received early in 1934. *Walter Davenport, "Money in the Mail Box," Colliers (February 10, 1934), 10-11, 47-48. Reprinted by permission.*

A pallid young woman with a cast-iron marcel, crimson finger nails and much more chewing gum than she needed jabbed a button or two and pulled a small lever. A shining tower of cams, pinions, ratchets, wheels, rods and plates in front of her began to mesh, mingle, slide and sing. A bit disdainfully she picked up a handful of cards which a mechanical carrier had fetched to her right hand and thrust them into the machine's mouth.

Promptly the contraption began to disgorge thin cardboard checks for men, women and estates in thirty states. . . .

In a couple of days they would be delivered to 10,000 villages, crossroads and lane ends and into the heavy hands of farmers who raise the country's wheat, cotton, tobacco, corn and hogs, and so on. At full speed, working twenty-four hours, 45,000 checks a day. And before the job could be finished these singing machines would have given to those farmers at least $600 million in bonuses, loans, grants and binders. Before it's all done it probably will be much more.

Far down Pennsylvania Avenue, on Capitol Hill, the knobby fingers of Congress are pointing in the direction of this granite building where we stand watching a river of gold rush through this granite canyon. Down there the noise is pretty loud. This, some insist, will ruin us all. Others contend that it is but half enough. What about the pecan growers, the beet farmers, the hop, poultry, asparagus, tomato, sheep, fish and soybean men? Answer us that! . . .

Let us stick to what we see. We've seen these farm checks made. To get it all we ought to follow them—let's say westward. The cotton and tobacco men have received theirs. Let's go west where there are still things to see and where there is still plenty of room to roam in. . . .

It was on a Wednesday that Mr. Lundborg's check arrived. If he had been the sort of man that kidding discomfited he would have been in quite a dither because all his neighbors had received theirs and had already undergone the mental strain of deciding what to do with the money, not that there weren't more uses to put it to than there were dollars.

But Mr. Lundborg was not a nervous man. For more years than he cared to think about he had raised hogs and corn under a Dakota sky, which could blister Satan himself in the summer and be frozen granite from Thanksgiving to May Day. Mr. Lundborg had learned to wait; Nature had taught him. Droughts had shriveled him and locusts had devoured him. Poland China hogs—waddling, snuffling mammoths—and Hampshires, too, had curled up on him overnight to die like babies in a black pestilence and he hadn't bothered so much as to learn the queer name of the thing that killed them. Such incidentals to a farmer's life as tax collectors and mortgage holders had besieged him and he hadn't even asked them how much they wanted. What would be the use? He wouldn't have it. The fatalistic Mr. Lundborg's veins ran full with patience.

So he knew that sooner or later the government was going to send him exactly $455—something more than half of it right away and the rest a year hence—and he wasn't to be flustered by all this nonsense. . . .

Rather than compile a schedule of the things he intended to buy, Mr. Lundborg had gone in for checking off what he wouldn't do. He owed the bank money, for example. But the bank owed him some, too. Last March his bank shut up tighter than a state's witness and nobody strong enough had come along to pry it open—nor foolish enough to try. So let the bank go chase itself with its conservator in it. He owed taxes too; but who didn't? He had been hearing a lot about taxes lately, although he suspected that something more than 99 per cent of what he had heard wasn't so.

Anyway he had heard that some were going to be written off and some rewritten and that Congress was going to do something about them. So his taxes wait a while despite the moans of local politicians that local government would cease to function if taxes weren't forthcoming from the landowners. As far as Mr. Lundborg was concerned it could go ahead and stop functioning, if it hadn't already. Let government find a way for him to sell his corn and hogs at a fair exchange price—say 60 cents a bushel and 7 or 8 cents a pound—and he would pay taxes. Besides, what did they mean—"landowners"? Between the bank, the tax collector and the owners of his mortgages he had lost grip on about everything but the door-latch of the house he lived in. And that was pretty loose.

So when the check arrived, Mr. Lundborg did precisely what most of his neighbors had done. He converted that card into cash. And believe him, that cash felt good. Understand this: I am not citing Mr. Lundborg because he departs from the ordinary but rather because in all essentials he is frankly representative of so many corn-belt farmers. And as far as his grasp of the general situation goes he is completely representative of Wisconsin's dairymen, Philadelphia's lawyers, New York's stockbrokers, Oklahoma's oilmen, Washington's lumbermen, California's fruit growers and North Carolina's weavers. He just limps along with the rest of us, hoping he's headed in the right direction.

Planning a Spending Spree

But with the actual money in his capacious hand, Mr. Lundborg called the family together. And after considerable argument, Mrs. Lundborg handed down the family decision. She usually does. The situation had been gone over in great detail. . . .

The north side of the house was no longer winter-proof. The wind had lost all respect for that side of their home and had become as familiar with the inside of the house as it was with the outside. Mr. Lundborg nodded. Thirty dollars for lumber. Out in the barn he already had enough nails to build a courthouse. Next.

Well, they wouldn't have to spend much for foodstuffs. The Lundborgs and their neighbors might be stony broke but it would be a long time before they starved. In the barn, the smokehouse, the cellar, attic and in sundry side rooms and closets there was food enough to keep the township well nourished for a year—pork, beef, dried and canned vegetables, potatoes, apples, home-ground flour and so on, not overlooking several five-gallon kegs of applejack to thaw out the interior of Mr. Lundborg after a frigid day in the fields. But they would be needing such things as sugar, coffee, salt and the like, which even so capable a man as Mr. Lundborg could not coax out of his corn-belt acres. So much for that.

As for the children—the young ones—well, Rolf was going to get a suit of clothes. Rolf, upwards of twelve now, had never been the proprietor of a whole suit of clothes. In fact, Rolf had never owned a pair of pants that had always been his. The only breeches he had ever worn were reach-me-downs converted from the remains of what some older male in the family had outgrown. Not that Rolf cared much. Were the decision left to him he would have chosen a bicycle or a radio; but Mrs. Lundborg was making the decisions and Rolf as well as his father had learned that counter-proposals were just so many wasted words. Moreover, and somewhat to the surprise of Mr. Lundborg, she now had the money in her hand. The money in one hand, a pencil in the other and thinking hard—that was Mrs. Lundborg. So her husband merely nodded at appropriate moments.

But a little later he contributed a few words. Let's see: There was lumber for the house, staple groceries for the pantry, so much to the grocer on that old bill, store clothes for the children, spectacles for young Anne, who had needed them a year, a subscription to the newspaper because these were no times to be going around unaware, several new parts for the motor car, two barrels of white paint and one of red, something on that seed loan. And so on until Mr. Lundborg called a halt. . . .

So on Saturday Mr. and Mrs. Lundborg drove to town alone. Leaving Mrs. Lundborg on West Main Street where the shops begin, he sauntered over to Steve's Southpaw Shave Shop where, to his amazement, he found six farmers ahead of him.

"I was sort of expecting you, Mr. Lundborg," said Steve. "I was just saying yesterday it was almost time for Mr. Lundborg to have his hair cut."

Mr. Lundborg was silently reading Steve's framed price list. It informed him that one could have one's hair cut, be shaved, singed, massaged, shampooed and all but drowned in bay rum for one dollar and seventy-five cents.

"I'm taking the works," said Mr. Lundborg.

"The whole card?" demanded Steve. "Why, Mr. Lundborg—"

"It's fifteen years since a barber shaved me," said Mr. Lundborg. . . .

You have to understand this about Lundborg: he might have been a bit more concerned about his taxes and his indebtedness for machinery, seed and mortgage interest had be turned to land speculation along with so many of his brethren back in the postwar years. . . .

Here's a farmer who, before the war, was doing well enough on 160 acres of corn. Since then he and the banks went crazy. Farm acres doubled and trebled in price, but not in value. . . . This fellow had bought land at $200, $300 and $400 an acre until, presently, he owned 1,600 acres.

That fellow isn't having his face massaged and he isn't taking his women folks to the movies in new coats either. He has had a series of nervous collapses. The bank that lent him the money to buy those additional acres has closed and promises to stay closed. But the owners of his mortgages and the tax collector are completely alive and growing more insistent. His check went to them and to seed loans and machine agencies. And he's still buried in debt.

And a curious thing about him is his resentment of the agreement he had to sign before being eligible to government bounty. To get that loan he had to agree to reduce his acreage by 20 per cent. Where he raised 1,400 acres of corn he must now plant no more than 1,120. And even that's too much.

Anyway, he resents it. It's his land—all of it, says he, and he works it hard and intelligently. Well, that's right enough. But he insists the government has no right to tell him how much he shall plant. Surplus of corn? Well, there shouldn't be any surplus. The trouble, he continues, is in distribution, not production. There are people in the cities starving for his corn and there it is in yellow hills wasting in his fields. Let the government buy it and give it to the hungry; then there wouldn't be all this surplus nonsense. The man grows furious as he talks—frightened, too, as he thinks of the future of his acres. What he wants is a fair exchange price, not limitation of crops. This limitation idea is contrary to nature and when government tries to buck nature —look out.

But he, like more than 90 per cent of the rest of the farmers, signs the crop reduction contracts which include hogs too. Under his borrowing agreement he must reduce the number of hogs he raises by 25 per cent. Moreover, he may not permit another to produce corn or hogs on land owned, rented or controlled by himself unless it, too, is covered by such a corn-hog contract. All this the government demands in its endeavor to reduce next year's production and cut down that destroying surplus of food.

This man is hooked hard because he had so many acres, because he paid so much for them, because his equity in his beautiful, high-priced fields is so small that they threaten to slip through his fingers. To listen to him you'd think him a firebrand radical. A few years ago when he was amassing this magnificence around him he talked like big business. Harken to his argument:

"The hell with Wallace, Peek, Tugwell and the rest of them down in Washington. What we farmers want is prices—60 cents for corn, a dollar for wheat, $8 a hundred pounds for hogs, 30 cents a pound for butter fat."

Some of his more philosophical neighbors like to bait him.

"Where are you going to get these prices? Who's going to pay them?"

"The government."

"What's the government going to do with it?"

"Let Wallace and Tugwell work that out. They're telling me what to do now, ain't they?"

"Suppose the government runs out of money?"

"Let them get it from Wall Street," roars this man, whose troubles were redoubled by land speculation.

"Suppose Wall Street ain't got it or won't come through?"

"Well, let's print it, by God—print plenty and break their backs."

But these of course are words of desperation. The man's pressed too hard, in a mental condition not conducive to calm thinking. However, if you persist, he will cool off enough to concede that the hole he is in is not as deep as it was last fall. For the land he agrees to keep out of production he gets what the government calls a rental at the rate of 30 cents a bushel, the number of bushels being calculated on past production. For example, let's take a little fellow who has taken twenty acres of corn off the market. His acres have been producing forty bushels each. He gets a rental or bonus of $12 an acre for keeping them out of cultivation. The government asks that he keep this land physically fit, however, using it for summer fallowing inasmuch as it is likely to be a bit tired anyway, or for pasture or meadow. This agreed to, the government grants him $240, two-thirds of which he gets at once and the balance a year hence. Like money in the bank —a good bank.

Similarly he gets a bonus for agreeing to reduce the number of hogs he will market this year—1934. He has agreed, let's say, to market only seventy-five hogs whereas he used to sell a hundred—at a loss. The government will make all that up to him by giving him $5 a head on the seventy-five he markets. Moreover, he gets two of those five dollars immediately and the other three in instalments. All told, therefore, he gets $310 in his first check.

Thus the 350 millions the government is giving to the corn-hog farmer to tide him over his most evil days. He may borrow, too, on foodstuffs he wishes to hold for the rising market that is predicted. But I met too many who were refusing to borrow to convince me that this offer from the government is completely popular. One of the crops that must be reduced, say the Lundborgs, is debts.

The farm women are having quite a lot to say about the spending of the money—and a very good idea too. In Iowa a farmer told me that he had had several high-grade ideas about getting rid of it, all of them pleasant, but that his wife had waved him aside from most of them.

"What we're doing," said he, "is pretty sensible, damn it. Personally I'm pretty tired of trying to be sensible, but my wife isn't. She says she hasn't had a chance to be sensible for so long that it's a luxury. So we're paying back what it cost us to put in our latest crop and paying our personal taxes. Personal taxes, mind. We're sort of letting the land tax slide, waiting to see what's going to happen in Washington and at the state capital. We're letting the mortgage ride along too. These mortgages will have to be written down some, I guess. I'd have a new car right away if I had my way but I guess she's right. We're paying up our store debts and laying in feed for the chickens that are going to help carry us through the winter. Sensible stuff. But a radio wouldn't go bad either. However, she says there isn't enough nourishment in a radio just now. But I got her to agree to one later. I'm letting her have her way with this first check, but the second one is going to be spent by the head of the house—me."

In the cities one hears lots of stuffy talk about the farmer and his government grants. It is usually inaccurate or aggrieved. It derives from two sources—one the professional politician who would tell you that the government should have stipulated that the state and the banks should have what amounts to liens on the money; and the other from the economist who bemoans the fact that Washington did not go the full distance and lay out scientific schedules of spending which, of course, would have included the purchasing of a number of things for which the farmer would have no particular use. The cities are full of self-anointed authorities on the farm problem. That they may be colossal failures in their own affairs seems not to deter them from attacking the farmer's.

One of the wisest of the politicians I met happens to be a state chairman—Republican. A few weeks ago he was asked by his superiors in the party to make a tour of his state and take note of such situations and tendencies as would be useful in a general onslaught on the Roosevelt administration, the object being to start operations in the current Congress and groom for the campaign for next fall's elections.

He learned something startling before going far. He says he had expected it for some time but now has the facts if not documentary proof. What irritated him more than the facts was that he had not been consulted—or at least notified. At any rate, he found that certain particularly hot members of two of the farm organizations had been accepting retainers from bankers who happened incidentally to be anti-Roosevelt. Just racketeers, you see.

"For this," he explained, "they were supposed to keep the farmers in a ferment, pitching into the Administration and declining to be pacified with anything short of immediate and permanent price fixing —which of course would be impossible—a wholesale write-off of debts or government assumption thereof and things like that. The curious thing about it is that some of these subsidized agitators went at it with considerable sincerity. They should have known better—known their farmers better.

"Such schemes are hatched in cities by men who must think the farmer a fool in spite of the protests of understanding and affection they profess for him. I have written to the gentleman who asked me to make this survey and have told him that if he wants to help the Roosevelt program a lot and end whatever chance the Republicans have of gaining a few congressional seats next fall, he should come out here himself and make a few speeches to the farmers bawling out the President and reminding the wheat and corn-hog country how beneficent the Hoover administration was. I have been active in politics out here for twenty-five years—always as a Republican. But I haven't known nor has anything in history taught me of any President who has caught and held the imagination of the farmer as Franklin Roosevelt has. These farmers believe in him, are willing to follow him wherever he leads, and God help the man who tries to drag them back toward the old order."

There is very little solace . . . for the anti-Roosevelt crowd in this situation. All that the farmer cares is that he has been rescued, temporarily at least, from grinding poverty. His morale has been strengthened not just with money but by the conviction that at last he is considered by Washington to be as important—perhaps even more important—than the capitalist and at last government is being administered in his interests. The pyramid has been inverted.

✔ **8. Tightening the cotton belt.** The effects of the AAA crop reduction program upon the poverty-stricken sharecroppers and other small farmers growing cotton in the South was far from what the New Dealers had envisaged. Webster Powell and Addison T. Cutler reported in *Harper's* at the end of the 1933 crop season upon conditions that grew even worse in the next year or two. *Webster Powell and Addison T. Cutler, "Tightening the Cotton Belt,"* Harper's *(February 1934), 308-16.*

The Southern cotton farmer has long been accustomed to suffering. He is now suffering farm relief. What he faces is sharply and authoritatively expressed by Assistant Secretary of Agriculture Rexford G. Tugwell, who said on August 4th, "We must study and classify American soil, taking out of production not just one part of a field or farm, but whole farms, whole ridges, perhaps whole regions. . . . It has been estimated that when lands now unfit to till are removed from cultivation, something around two million persons who now farm will have to be absorbed by other occupations."

A glance at Southern agriculture will show what the Agricultural Adjustment Administration has stepped into, for better or for worse. . . .

Cotton growing in the southeastern section of the cotton belt— the Carolinas, Georgia, and Alabama—is based upon the labor of sharecroppers, Negro and White. Planters and merchants refer to them as "niggers" and "poor whites" just as they did "before the War between the States." To a large extent, the plantations of the Mississippi delta also depend upon croppers, although the increasing use of tractors up to the depression brought with it a partial shift to wage labor. The newer cotton areas of Texas and Oklahoma, however, are largely operated by tenant farmers who pay one-third or one-fourth of the crop as rent to an absentee landlord. They enjoy a farmer's independence in tilling the soil but submit to a farmer's dependence upon the credit and marketing institutions with which they must deal.

Last summer as we drove along dusty roads between rows of waving cotton, white and green, the bolls were just bursting open in the late August sun. On each fifteen- or twenty-acre patch stood a board cabin, containing one room and a kitchen, unpainted and unchinked against the winter frosts. In these cropper cabins live families of five or more; the average is seven. Working in the cotton patch at the doorstep could be seen the whole family, from six to sixty. Their clothing was a patchwork of old scraps sewn together. Bare feet were the rule, relieved occasionally by rude sandals made of bits of burlap bagging. An old straw sombrero topped the costume. Beside the cabin lay the cotton which had been plowed under by government persuasion—enough cotton to clothe this family and many other farm families. It lay on the black earth yet no one dared pick it.

The sharecroppers are regarded by the landlord-masters as a class of labor rather than as tenant farmers, although the cropper's legal status is that of a propertyless tenant. He and his family grow ten to twenty acres of cotton and sometimes plant a little corn and a small garden. The land, the mule, plow, and other equipment are supplied by the landlord, who in addition usually keeps the family alive during the growing season by advances of rations. At the end of the year the crop is supposed to be divided equally between the landlord and the cropper. The theory is that the landlord's half is rent for the use of his land and equipment, while the cropper's half is the return for his labor. That is the relationship in theory and law. It is illustrated by the common expression in the South to describe a cropper. He is "working on halves," they say. But in fact the proceeds of the whole of the crop, when it is sold, go to the landlord. This is because the landlord simply takes the cropper's half to pay for the monthly advances of rations which the cropper has received during the growing season, together with the interest thereon. The rations are the traditional slave diet—"fatback," meal, and molasses. It is well known that no matter what the yield and price of cotton, the cropper is usually still in debt to the landlord at the end of the year. In fact he is often farther in debt than he was at the same time the preceding year. The landlord keeps the books. . . .

This Southern pattern of social relations between landlord and cropper has made it possible for the landlord to pass a maximum of loss to the cropper, as the price of cotton has tumbled in recent years. Low standards of living have become even lower. Apparently the limit is a matter of calories only. The average annual furnishings supplied by landlords to croppers this year was $50 to $60. This applies to the Southeast and Mississippi areas and is based on statements made to us by landlords, croppers, and local officials. For a family of five this amounts to about 3 cents per person per day. The total income of course may be augmented somewhat by odd jobs picked up during the winter or by a few vegetables grown in the garden. Cropper gardens, any Southerner will tell you, are "no account." The small income usually allotted to the cropper from the sale of cotton seed was absent this year because the value of that byproduct was absorbed by the increased cost of ginning. . . .

The reasons which influenced the decision to "plow under" are clear. A 13,000,000 bale carry-over from the preceding crop year— equal to a year's crop—threatened a price for 1933 even lower than the disastrous 1932 price of 5 to 6 cents per pound. Large plantation owners had made it clear that under the most "efficient" conditions profits could not be made at a price of 5 cents, not to mention a lower price. Farm creditors, including banks, merchants, insurance companies, and the government itself, faced a complete cessation of returns from farmers. (That this factor was a strong one, perhaps the strongest one, in influencing the decision is suggested by the fact that the actual benefits of the plan went in large measure to the creditors, as will be later shown.) Finally it was emphatically represented at a conference of interested parties held in Washington on June 3rd by the Agricultural Adjustment Administration that unless something was done, the social unrest in the South would be so great that "property would not be safe."

The plowing-up campaign was opened with much publicity in the latter part of June. As an inducement for plowing up cotton, the government offered a sliding scale of benefit payments depending on the prospective yield of the cotton acreage plowed under. The payment was to take the form of cash or of part cash and part option on government-owned cotton. When the campaign proved to be lagging it was extended into July. It was run, at the top, by the cotton section of the Agricultural Adjustment Administration. Next came the extension directors of the state agricultural colleges. Below them were the county agents, who are paid jointly by the state and the federal Department of Agriculture. Although their usual task is to give farmers scientific information on how to be efficient in increasing production, this time their job was to persuade farmers to plow up about one quarter of the best crop they had seen in years.

The county agent was the local keyman in the campaign. He appointed a county committee, composed of the leading big farmers. The county committees appointed local committees. The instructions to these committees were to "sell" the scheme to all the farmers of the county, to get them to sign the contracts with the government, and to pass on how much acreage and yield per acre the farmer could claim when it came to the government benefit payments. These benefit payments opened the door to all sorts of petty local graft and favoritism. Exactly how much of it there was will probably never be known. We do know that some farmers refused to serve on the committee, saying that if they were strictly honest in the appraisals they would lose some of their friends. In the hundreds of counties we visited we did not find a single case where a sharecropper or a representative of the poorer ranks of farmers was put on the committee.

The campaign was pushed by methods of high-pressure salesmanship, similar to those of the NRA campaign in industry which followed closely after. First was the attempt to convince the cotton farmer that he would benefit himself by signing up. Of course it was seen that the payments for the plowed-up cotton would probably not amount to as much as the sale of that cotton if it were allowed to reach the market. But still it amounted to something. . . .

When the smoke and dust of the campaign had subsided it was found that the small farmers had almost all taken the "straight cash" plan while the big farmers and plantation owners had chosen the option plan. This was because the small farmers felt that they needed the cash immediately, that they could not afford to wait for the probably greater benefits under the option plan. They also distrusted the option plan as savoring of stock exchanges. They failed to realize then that their government checks would in any event be swallowed up by their creditors. It was also found that very few sharecroppers had signed up with the government. Their landlords usually just signed up for them.

By the time the cotton farmer was notified by his county agent that his contract was accepted by the government and that it was permissible to go ahead with the plowing-up it was well along in July. This meant that in most cases it was too late to plant a feed crop on the plowed-up acreage. (The government would not allow the farmer to plant a cash crop on it.) It also meant that in many sections the cotton was mature. So when the farmer did his thorough job of turning under the cotton plants, the bolls opened and lay white on the ground. This caused a good deal of discussion among farmers. Signing up in the midst of a patriotic campaign was one thing, but actually plowing up the cotton they had sweated to grow was another. Most of them said it was too bad to plow it up when people were going ragged. They frequently mentioned that people were going ragged in their own community. "Why didn't the government buy the cotton and give it to the needy?" they asked. Many of them said that it looked as if there was something pretty crazy somewhere. They were puzzled to know what had brought about the craziness and eagerly inquired for diagnoses even from Yankee travelers passing through.

There was also widespread dissatisfaction with the delay, because by the time they were told to plow up, the farmers found the plants grown so high that it was difficult to destroy them effectively. There was no farm lore about the technic of plowing-up. Some of the plants would start growing again after they had been once plowed under. The government was very strict about a thorough destruction of the plants. "Render the cotton unfit for picking," was the order. . . .

The protection of the farmer's private creditor had been planned from the very beginning. At the time when John Doe signed the plow-up contract with the government he was required to list any creditors who held a first mortgage on his crop. When the checks finally arrived from Washington they included the creditor as joint payee. A holder of a second mortgage on John's crop was not automatically protected in this way. He was made joint payee only if he had attended to his own interests by means of getting John to insert a clause in the contract entitling him to appear as payee on the check. Many of the second mortgage holders did this. Others who were lax in this respect at the time the contracts were being signed pestered the county agents to look out for their interests. As a result of all this, many farmers never saw a penny in cash for the good cotton they had plowed up.

Whether the sharecropper received any payment or any credit allowance for the cotton plowed up on his patch depended upon the tender mercies of his landlord. The situation can best be described by quoting from a county agent in a big cotton county in the Mississippi delta. This agent said that he made all arrangements for the government with the landlords, and the landlords simply agreed with him to treat the croppers "right." His attitude toward the croppers as well as that of the landlords is shown by the following statement: "You know, the government in Washington caused us quite a little trouble here. By mistake they mailed some of the checks made out to nigger croppers. They probably didn't know what they were doing when they did it. Imagine giving a check to a nigger cropper! Of course, I turned these checks over to the landlords anyhow. They'll have to get the croppers to endorse them before they take them to the bank. But that won't be hard."

The upshot of the above is that the government seemed more anxious to help creditors collect their debts than to give farmers a little purchasing power. Otherwise the government would have refused to give creditors any lien on these checks on the ground that this was an emergency relief program.

If the success of the Administration's cotton program were to be gauged exclusively by price changes, without regard to the division of the proceeds, very little, if any, positive achievement can be credited to the plan. The price of cotton was lifted during the plow-up campaign to a high point of about 12 cents per pound. The reaction, however, carried it down to a low point of $7\frac{1}{2}$ cents per pound at the opening of the market season, when some cotton farmers started disposing of their new crop. The price was about $9\frac{1}{2}$ cents in late September when the first rumblings of renewed farm discontent reached government ears. The President's announcement that the new crop could be used as security for government loans at 10 cents per pound wherever promises of future acreage reduction were given kept the price from going below the 10 cent level.

In the meantime, however, the combination of NRA, processing taxes, and currency depreciation was boosting the price of the commodities which farmers buy. The common complaint which we heard from farmers in all sections of the cotton South during the summer was that the price of flour had literally doubled within the span of three months and overalls had jumped from 49 cents to $1.00. These two items appeared to symbolize all the concentrated feelings of outrage over the rising cost of living. The degree of success of the general efforts of the Administration to restore agricultural prices to prewar "parity" may be judged by the official indexes of farm prices corrected for prices paid by farmers. The resultant index, called "farm purchasing power," stood at 61 (with 1910 to 1914 as 100) on May 15th when the Farm Act was passed. On July 15th it had risen to 71; but by September 15th it had fallen back to 60. The situation was frankly admitted by Secretary Wallace when he declared, according to *The New York Times* of September 9th, that "increased retail costs have taken up the farmer's additional income and left him no better off for meeting his interest, taxes and fixed charges."

Whatever small groups may have benefited from the Administration's cotton program, it is quite clear that millions of people have paid the cost of it. The processing tax is paid by all consumers of cotton goods, including unemployed as well as employed city workers and including farmers themselves, who also wear cotton shirts and overalls.

There is, however, serious reason to believe that the real cost of the cotton-reduction program does not end with the processing tax. Does not the shrinkage in the agricultural "plant" involve a shrinkage in agricultural personnel, thus adding to the problem of unemployment? Assistant Secretary Tugwell's remark, quoted at the beginning of this article, certainly suggests that in the long view it is not only a definite possibility, but actually part of the general plan for agriculture. On the other hand it must be recognized that the Administration hoped, at least, that the 1933 plow-up would not cause the separation of sharecroppers from their meager livelihood. The printed instructions issued to the field agents managing the plow-up campaign included the following item: "Local committees should make every effort to influence plantation operators to make an equitable arrangement with their tenants so as not to discharge some of their tenants for the remainder of the year as a result of the reduction in acreage."

The absence of large-scale dismissal of sharecroppers as a result of the cotton plow-up of 1933 cannot be attributed to the efforts of the local committees as much as to another and more accidental factor. Acreage reduction, coming late in the season and taking the form of plowing up nearly mature cotton, provided much less inducement to landlords to dismiss their croppers than would have been the case if the program had been applied at the beginning of the growing season.

Since a large part of the expense of raising the crop, including advances of rations to croppers, had already been incurred, the landlord was disposed to keep all his croppers. If some of the cotton patches would yield no harvest to pick, the landlord, nevertheless, wanted the croppers to "work out" in some other way the money already spent on them.

We have stated the rule. There were numerous exceptions. We encountered a number of cases where the landlord arranged with the government to plow up all of the patch operated by an individual cropper and followed this up by closing the books with the cropper and sending him "down the road." This happened most often in the Mississippi delta, which is characterized by large plantations worked by as many as fifty cropper families. The story, as told by the ex-croppers themselves, is that the boss plowed up their cotton and stopped furnishing them, *i.e.* stopped the weekly advances which in fact amount to a wage envelope for a cropper, although a small one. The boss would generously allow the cropper to stay in his cabin while searching for a job at picking cotton.

In Texas, where cotton is grown chiefly by tenants of a higher economic standing than sharecroppers and where cotton is picked by wage earners, the government plan had the definite effect of reducing the employment of cotton pickers. This created a serious problem. Local authorities and relief agencies did not know what to do with the transient labor. Whole families, hitchhiking, driving in rattletrap cars, or even in covered wagons, were shunted from one community to another. They had heard about the prospects of a fine crop this year and had come early, from the towns in south Texas and the East, only to find that as much as half the crop had been plowed up on some of the farms. Negroes and Mexicans, who had obtained picking jobs in past years, found that picking jobs were being reserved for "local white farmers." Transients were not entitled to local relief. At the beginning of the picking season the order went out from the state relief committee to stop all work relief during picking time in order not to "demoralize" labor.

The signs of much larger displacement and unemployment for 1934 are truly ominous. In 1934 it will not be a question of sending croppers "down the road" in the middle of the season. It will be a question of the landlord's failing to renew his verbal contracts with the tenants. That the landlords have been thinking along these lines is evidenced by the fact that they have been delaying the renewal of their tenant contracts until the 1934 reduction plan is made clear. In all parts of the South where the cropper system predominates it is regarded as certain that the problem of cropper displacement will be much more serious in 1934. Landlords, croppers, county agents, and agricultural experts all spoke to us freely and emphatically on this point when the question was raised. Why should the landlord go to the expense of keeping a sharecropper working land which is no longer devoted to the raising of cotton? The government will not allow other cash crops to be raised on reduced cotton acreage for fear of spoiling the market for these crops. It is not, perhaps, unfair to recall at this point the insistence of many Southern white people that the Negro sharecropper is fitted for nothing but the raising of cotton.

Of course, no one can predict how many cropper families will be told to move out. That will depend upon soil conditions, the income of individual landlords and their feeling toward the cropper families, and the guess of particular planters as to the price of cotton during the next few years. Some croppers will remain on the land, left to their own devices to wrest a meager living from the skimpy soil which the landlord considers worthless. Others will be evicted from the land in order to enable the landlords to use every inch of soil and to get rid of upkeep on leaky, dilapidated cabins—possibly in order to escape the unpleasant necessity of passing by starving families every day. In some cases croppers will be given fewer acres to work.

A Growing Emphasis Upon Reform

Throughout the New Deal there ran a thread of reform which, from the nature of the movement, grew in emphasis from 1933 into 1937. President Roosevelt upon taking office viewed his task as involving, first, the achievement of recovery and, second, the passage of reform legislation to make future depressions less likely. At the very outset Congress passed one of the major reform measures, the establishment of the Tennessee Valley Authority. Some other measures, long planned, like Social Security, were not enacted for several years. Among the New Dealers and from millions of underprivileged people throughout the country there was pressure for greater and greater reform, which undoubtedly helped make this the dominant theme of the Roosevelt program from 1935 to 1937.

9. **The dimensions of TVA.** Throughout the twenties Senator George Norris had fought for government development of the electric power going to waste at Wilson Dam on the Tennessee River. Even before he took office, President Roosevelt pledged his support to Norris' proposal, and even went further to authorize in the Tennessee Valley Authority an experiment in regional resource development and social planning. *Fortune* in 1935 analyzed many facets of the emergent TVA program in a lengthy study, a part of which follows. *"TVA,"* Fortune (*May 1935*), *93-98, 140-162. Copyright © 1935 by Time, Inc. Reprinted by permission of* Fortune *Magazine.*

Two million Americans live in the Tennessee Valley—a patch of world the size of England. Here is a characteristic union of land and water and wealth—immense potentialities that man has quite as characteristically misused to his own disadvantage. This combination of potentiality and past misuse makes of the valley a sovereign proving ground for industrial and social history.

That arduous proof is in the hands of the Tennessee Valley Authority. Well worthy of watching is this Authority, since at its best it could bring to the people of the nation a new wisdom in the use of their continent, and at its worst, still stands high in promise.

To what degree the Authority will ever fulfill its gigantic hopes is not for consideration here. The next five years, the next ten, may prove little. The next twenty, the next seventy, much. In the meantime, nevertheless, two examinations of the present status of TVA are worth undertaking for their own sake. One consideration is of the intention as a whole and of the accomplishment to date, and that begins herewith. The other consideration is of the issue that is currently the sharpest—so sharp indeed that it may cripple the whole endeavor. And that is Power, and the battle over Power, and the national significance of the battle. . . .

The mountains and blue lapsing hills are encysted with time-wrought wealth: coal and iron by the thousands of millions and limestone and fat clays by the billions of tons, and bauxite and copper and zinc and manganese and barytes and mica and olivine and kyanite and silky talc and, in all, not less than forty of the minerals most useful to mankind. All these await, for the most part, cheap power and the new processes that cheap power will make feasible. And the silver rivers yellowing and widening with weight of clay, which bind this valley into unity deeper than man can fence his states; a linkage and veinage of moving waters ill-kempt for navigation, capable of apoplectic flood, but muscled with a munificence of power that man has scarcely touched.

Steep land planted to corn, runneled and ruined with rain; flat land planted to cotton, worn and warped like a wrecked heel. A new season spreading its smoke on the air and its health on the earth. Cities that you would describe as provincial; towns you would describe as rube; farms so pitiable you would be sure to laugh at them. In fact if tall talk has led you to believe that by now TVA must already have changed the face of its valley, you are much mistaken. It is the same with the valley's two million people.

Yet they are all very well aware that TVA is at work. As for their several attitudes, they're precisely what you might expect. Every man is most interested in himself. A Knoxville businessman who was born and raised upstate feels TVA may talk a good deal but that anything TVA can do to raise the standard of living is all to the good. A Lafollette undertaker to whom has fallen the job of removing several hundreds of the coffins, at $20 a shot, from the Norris Reservoir area, holds that TVA is doing a fine work. A Knoxville marble man is not so sure about the wisdom and efficiency of his government. Here is TVA babbling all manner of bright talk about putting the valley on its feet: here on the other hand are Morgenthau and Ickes asserting that of the millions to go into new public buildings, not a dollar shall be "wasted" in making "mausoleums" of them—calmly slitting the throat, in fact, in the name of economy, of one of the leading industries in a valley the government is spending still other millions to bring to life. The Mayor of Tupelo, on the other hand, is all smiles, and they are all genuine smiles, for his was the first of all towns to crouch at the brink of TVA's cheap power, and drink. A sharecropper a few miles above Wheeler Dam, on still another hand, is anything but smiles: TVA has bought the land he farms right out from under him; he gets no money; what is he to do?

And so on. Speaking more generally: Republican families in the northeastern mountains are all but convinced that Democrats are capable of honest intentions. In such dealings as they have had, they have found TVA no sucker and no bleeder; eager with suggestion; carefully never officious in following it up. They are favorable; and still a little skeptical; they will wait and see. The people of the southwest are grateful to Mr. Roosevelt as for rain from heaven: for the first time since reconstruction, the government is paying them attention: this time, they are convinced, the attention is benevolent. The only real trouble: they are so eager for help that they forget to help themselves. They have repeatedly asked TVA to help them organize and to speak at demonstrations against the utilities—a thing which of

course TVA has had firmly to refuse. Just here, in fact, you approach
the core of one of TVA's major problems.

TVA knows that it is, among other things, a passel of smart Yankees descended to improve a tetchy people; knows also the limits of
its power; knows also that the more independently a man helps himself, the better off he is. For which wise reasons, TVA is most ex-
traordinarily shy of stepping over the line. It must, very delicately,
put ideas into valley heads; then sit tight and wait for the valley to
come and ask. What TVA also knows but may not realize seriously
enough—such realization may be impossible—is that generations of
poverty and habit breed a quite indescribable inertia; that hopeful and
faintly skeptical apathy and an almost childlike dependence are in
general very possibly the liveliest attitudes that can be hoped for without very considerable guidance from above. And granted even that,
are your troubles over? When all is said and done, the real crux of
the problem is simpler and more cruel: ideas are practiced by and
upon human beings, who fulfill them only more or less workably,
never perfectly. The better the idea, the more inevitable the compromise.

So much, in a broad-spoken way, for the valley and its people. As
for the people who are responsible for carrying out the enormously
ambitious and complex job that is TVA, there are, in all, some 12,000
of them. You may see them swarming like mites on the rising bulk of
Norris Dam, of Wheeler Dam; buying and clearing and damming the
steep land long miles above those dams and burning all brush so that
even the soft May landscape sours with autumnal smoke; boring into
the earth and stone where Pickwick Landing Dam will rise; swathing
soft slopes of land with terraces; training up seedlings by the million,
the next forest generation; at watch in the huge white hall where
Wilson Dam broods power; at work in the phosphate lands and in the
monstrous nitrate-phosphate plant at the Shoals; at work in scores
and hundreds of offices—at Muscle Shoals (the official headquarters)
in officers' wartime quarters revised for business: at work in Chattanooga in the wild omelet of limestone which is the Old Post Office;
in ramshackle Temporary Building F in Washington, where none can
smoke and a director up on business can hang his hat; in Knoxville,
the field headquarters, in East Tennessee. Above all in smoky Knoxville, where 1,100 errand boys and typists and accountants and statis-
ticians and architects and geologists and geographers and pressmen
and lawyers and executives and coordinators and directors, crammed
into five office buildings, tend their Authoritative muttons.

For the best beginning, get up about seven (for Knoxville business starts at eight) and, after breakfast, walk up sooty Gay Street and turn down smudgy Union and on past Market Square straight on to the New Sprankle Building, a block this side of the Masonic Temple. Go upstairs and through the brisk bare corridors into one of the brisk bare offices and there, if you are lucky, you will find yourself face to face with the very men who run this show.

They are three: two of them soberly dressed, sixtyish, one rather sportily dressed, in his middle thirties. The man with the broad hands, the heavy, delicately cut aquiline head, is Dr. Arthur E. Morgan, one-time hydraulic engineer, famed President of Antioch College, and Chairman of the Board of Directors of the Tennessee Valley Authority. The man with the drawled, humorist's mouth and the stringy body of a farmer is Dr. Harcourt Morgan, onetime President of the University of Tennessee and a member of the Board of Directors; and if you would have him as he is you must temper that picture with light washes of cultivation and of city living. The quick-handed, quick-faced man is David Eli Lilienthal, who is one of the more brilliant of the Frankfurters who populate New Deal offices, who has seen service on the Wisconsin utilities front, and who is the third of the directors of TVA. When, in July 1933, these three men first met in the valley and set up their tent, they were three men alone, and their first task was to understand how their whole job hung together.

TVA is a corporation created by the Tennessee Valley Authority Act, which was Roosevelt's development on Senator Norris's hard-fought Shoals theme. It was granted by Congress an initial $50,000,-000 (appropriations total $75,000,000 to date, of which some $70,000,-000 is spent). Primarily, TVA is in the valley for the purpose of developing the Tennessee River system for navigation and flood control. That means, first of all, building dams. When you build a dam, however, a great many things happen at once.

In the first place, you back up water and you generate power. More power, a lot more perhaps, than you'll need to operate the locks, which are a part of your development-of-navigation program. It would be criminal waste not to make use of this surplus power. Therefore you sell it—to farmers, municipalities, industries.

Also when you build a dam, especially if it is in steep, loose-landed country, you must look to your reservoirs: you must bring erosion under control. The control of erosion breaks into two parts: reforestation and just plain erosion control. For the latter, if you are to grow healthy and tenacious cover crops, you need fertilizers; particularly you need phosphate fertilizers. With phosphate beds in the heart of the valley, with a plant to hand at Muscle Shoals, you make them and use them.

But you don't own all the land that drains into the river; farmers own most of it. Aside from your basic (and legalized) interest in the welfare of the farmer as a member of society, there is an entirely hardboiled reason why you should consider him seriously: potentially, he is a voracious power customer. He needs money to pay for his power; he also needs to be persuaded—as he best can be by an improved standard of living—that he wants and, indeed, needs it.

Good soil, planted right and kept good, will help enormously. Hence your expansion of the erosion-control program to include terracing, fertilizer, and planting demonstrations. But he can farm the land and more besides. Suppose, for instance, he learns to use and to market the natural resources that surround him. And suppose he can find part-time work in factories. Here, from several paths at once, you converge on industry.

The farmer needs extra money, extra work; TVA needs two kinds of customers: farmers and new industries. There is much to be said, to the advantage of everyone concerned, for a balancing of industry and agriculture. To certain types of industry—notably the electrochemical, the electrometallurgical—cheap power is of prime importance; it so happens that your valley is rich not merely in cheap power but in the very resources essential to those particular industries.

It therefore behooves you to study carefully those resources, to heel yourself, in fact, with every sort of information that may be of value to industrialists interested in setting up shop in the region. And to know your land and its people and all that is actual and potential in them, from stem to gudgeon: and so to determine each detail of their present that it shall build without waste or conflict into the future which is likewise your responsibility.

Here, then, assembled according to their more salient and simple interrelations, you have the several parts of a social-industrial-agrarious creature—or rather, the mirage of the whole creature it is your business to create. When you go about creating it you find out this in short order: TVA is authorized to build dams, to operate them, to sell power, to develop good fertilizers. Beyond that, TVA has no power whatever. TVA is authorized only to guide. It can be useful as a guide by having ready to hand information so valuable and so thorough and so patently wise and farsighted that industrialists and farmers can but use it as the best of all possible advice—and by working eternally in cooperation with county and state and federal agencies.

Here, if you like, is a difficult hole. Wouldn't it be far more convenient and to the point if, to be brief, TVA *owned* the valley and the people in it? The answer is, that it might indeed be far more convenient and to the point. There are many names for it these days, and

Socialism will do. The facts, again, are different. The way good work is done by a democratic government in the fourth decade of the twentieth century is the way TVA is doing it. . . .

Labor at the Wheeler Dam Site

A couple of matters swing into relevance here as they don't up at Norris. . . .

The Negro. With white men by the hundreds out of jobs, TVA very quietly, but very firmly in line with its policy, began hiring Negroes by tens and twenties until their employment percentage tallied with the population percentage in those parts: about 20 per cent. Having hired them it proceeded to pay them the same wages and gave them housing precisely as good as that of the whites and training perhaps better. (Reason for good training: there are swarms of first-rate Negroes out of work; a Ph.D., for instance, heads the Negro training staff.) Meanwhile such TVA men as know the country at first hand were set for anything up to and including a lynching. Nothing happened, and they figured out why. TVA, and the Negroes too, had sense enough to stick absolutely to Jim-Crowism, which isn't necessarily edifying but which feels better, at any moment, than bright coal oil and buckshot. Moreover, TVA's workmen had no longer to fear that their jobs would be washed from under them by cheap Negro labor; TVA wasn't taking that advantage, so commonly taken, either of its Negroes or of them. TVA ran foul of some objection on the part of leading citizens of local towns when it began training them toward a higher possible standard of living—but it reminded them (a) that neither intermarriage nor insurrection was being preached and (b) that the Negro was undeniably a member of the community and might better be a decent than an indecent one, and went on about its business.

The Sharecropper. He may be either white or black. The sharecropper who builds Wheeler Dam gets free and good training toward a better life; the sharecropper upstream who clears the reservoir gets more of the same and he and his neighbors get all the firewood they want to haul away, gratis. But you can't practice a proper rotation of crops if your job, as a tenant, is to wring the very gizzard of land you don't own with cotton and cotton and more of it. You're in an even worse hole if your plot is above the Wheeler site and TVA has to buy it from under you. Your landlord gets the money, all you get is moving orders. TVA does all it can, and has found new places for a good many tenants. But the sharecropper and the Negro are two profoundly painful problems that TVA, by no fault or oversight of its own, has no constitutional power either to solve or to get far under the skin of. Out of 230,000 farmers there are 95,000 tenants in the valley. Not enough, perhaps, to balk TVA's program; but enough to lift them beyond mere sentimental discussion.

Agricultural Planning

If the U.S. really learns to take care of its land, and really cares to preserve it for the future, it will be just about the first civilization that has done so, and the time is spoiled rotten for beginning. Not to mention great swaths of the continent at large that we have man-handled, consider merely the general South. These past four genera-tions, we have wrung the very blood from the land and shipped its health to market and seaward by the sewers and left it exhausted and misplanted for the rain to do the rest. Left to its own devices and the rain's, that whole land could be desert before another century had passed.

Or just take the Tennessee Valley. By quality and by geography, it breaks very roughly into three parts. By quality it is a third good, a third middling, a third godawful, nearly all in danger. Geographically: the east and north are steep, planted much to corn when planted at all, sickly most of it, rooked with gullies. The west and south are gentler sloping, wearied with a surfeit of cotton, slowly more sterile year by year, year by year quite surely sloughing its skin. In three or four of the middle counties there is land as rich as any on this con-tinent, and the wounds of rain heal swiftly level as the harmed flesh of a healthy child, for this land overlies phosphate beds. But else-where in the valley you would hardly set a camera down and fail to get some record of the great mange of the land.

So the jobs ahead of TVA are these: to save and to restore the land. To learn and to practice its best uses. To teach and guide and perhaps ultimately to distribute the farmers accordingly. If you think this could be nicely handled by Home Folks Unassisted, take the word of Mr. William M. Landess of the Agricultural Division: it can't. As county agent for Shelby County, Landess used to spend a day apiece at one farm after another, checking up on erosion and telling what to do about it. He figures that if he had kept on with that job alone, day by day, he would have been back for a second visit to his first farm at the end of fifteen years.

On slopes up to fifteen degrees, the first job is terracing. Terracing is a simple enough matter: you lay open, across the axis of a hill, a broad and shallow trough, with the lip of earth on the downhill side. How wide apart these troughs are laid depends, of course, on the slope and the soil. At the far ends you clean out permanent gullies, and check them with dams. It is no invention of TVA's; in fact TVA found a terracing program started in Alabama, an overworked county agent trying to run it. TVA called in all state agricultural representatives and together they drew up a procedure whereby TVA and the agencies work hand in glove, with funds chiefly under contract with the land-grant colleges of the states. The county commission or the terracing cooperative or the "club" of farmers and agents (the setup answers to several names) contracts for equipment at around $4,500 per unit, leases it from the manufacturer, liquidates the lease by charging $2.50 an hour for terracing, about half of which goes toward liquidation. When they started, just one company—Caterpillar Tractor—had the tractor-and-special-plough equipment they needed. Several others put it out now; farmers have watched four in the same field putting on a demonstration. Terracing doesn't cost much, and the secret of its cheapness is Diesel power. . . . Its cost is a fifth the running cost of the old gas tractor, farmers figure; and they figure too that thirty mules would do the same work at the same speed, more expensively. Twenty thousand farmers are involved. Of the ninety-nine farm counties in the valley, the Authority is concentrating its first attention on the seventy-five nearest the rivers, and that goes not merely for the terracing but for the whole agricultural program.

But terracing, even on feasibly gentle slopes, isn't the whole story. To get at some further extension of that story, turn to the east; in the valley east and north of Chattanooga.

Of its 14,000,000 acres, 8,000,000 are in farms. Of this 8,000,000 more than a third is in pasture, more than a third in small patches of woods, the rest—well under a third—is in crops. Of the crop land, about half is planted to corn. Plenty of that corn is planted on land steep as a cow's face—the steepest registers an all but incredible 88 per cent. Off every acre of that corn land, corn and steep soil being what they are, you lose thirty and forty tons of topsoil every year. As for the pasture land, that too is steadily weakening: the pasturage like a poultice withdraws the phosphorus and the lime from the soil; there is less for next year's plants to draw on; as the sods weaken the carrying season steadily shortens and the feeding period steadily lengthens out; first the legumes go, then the grass, then the land wastes swiftly open—a bare and spreading sore.

The wards of the key that will open this deadlock are two. One is in the roots of legumes, and the other is down at Muscle Shoals, at Nitrate Plant No. 2.

If good crops are to grow indefinitely, the soil needs plant food. Of lime, which sweetens the soil and the flesh of its produce, the valley reeks. Of potash, nearly all soil except numb sand has enough. Of nitrogen, you can get plenty by planting legumes—clover, peas, beans, alfalfa, vetches—which enlist nitrogen out of the free air and nail it into the land. But the phosphorus that you need to raise those legumes —or any other crop—is not so easy a story. All we need say here is that in shipping its grains and its meats to market and in committing its sewage to oblivion, civilization very steadily imposes an enormous and perhaps ultimately suicidal tax upon the land. And though in time we may learn to respect our sewage—attempts to extract phosphorus from it have been technically but not emotionally successful—and may learn also to wangle phosphorus out of sea water, the chief source still is the vast graveyard of those prehistoric beasts whose bones are thawed long since into the earth but whose burden of phosphorus has been processed by time into phosphate beds such as those to be found in Florida, in a few of the Western states, and in middle Tennessee.

The sequiturs, intensely in brief, are these: TVA is farming a number of the mid-state deposits, not by large-scale methods, wastefully, but by truck and shovel, sparingly: "phosphate farmers" must guarantee to put their land back into shape for cultivation after the mining, and are shown how. The phosphates are shipped to Nitrate Plant No. 2, at the Shoals. Where, by the end of last summer, TVA had completed a $65,000 experiment with a pocket-size blast furnace which was to develop data for the design of a small commercial-size unit. The designs for this in turn are now nearing completion.

Ordinary superphosphate runs 16 to 20 per cent plant food (P_2O_5). It is possible—but at too high a cost—to produce concentrates up to 52 per cent. The superphosphate TVA is producing analyzes at about 45 per cent, and the problems to be solved are two: the technical improvements that will bring down the cost to take advantage of an ultimate 25 per cent saving in cost of delivery; and the education of the farmer in the use of this new high-powered fertilizer. So far, TVA has produced some 7,000 tons. It is being distributed to Agricultural Experiment Stations, to demonstration farms, and for use in erosion control. Trading problems rear no ugly head as yet: distribution will be the same for a long time to come, and production will be geared accordingly. Notably, the fertilizer will go to some 2,000 demonstration farms—now being selected—all over the valley: and they will be not merely large-scale laboratories, but large-scale and highly variegated schoolrooms where the whole of farm practice will be studied and taught.

To sum up: TVA is very definitely committed to the extensive development of grazing lands and of livestock raising. In the east to hold steep soil in check; in the west to board the seesaw opposite the fat King Cotton; in all the valley to improve the land and to alter for the better the life of the farmer. TVA is also definitely committed to the attempt to break the one-crop system. TVA is also hopefully but less definitely committed to the effort to distribute the valley farmers upon land they can farm. Much of which is a long, long way off and TVA knows it well. The sharecropper is still one problem; the private ownership of land is another; the natural inertia of many a farmer, the backwardness of many another, are two more. Already TVA realistically knows that its moving-to-better-land must be done step by step: a man must have learned to farm mediocre land before you saddle him with excellence. So far, what the Agricultural Division has done in the way of action and demonstration is of necessity merely the fringe of a huge fabric ahead. If you want to see where it all leads to, you had best glance that way again six months and a year and ten from now. And if you are inclined already to pass judgment or to line up conjectures the only answer is don't.

Preparing to Sell Power

We should observe in passing that the two key states, Alabama and Tennessee, have during this past winter laid legislative tracks along which TVA can run into its new country—tracks laid and greased especially to facilitate the execution of the balkiest and only hard-fought part of TVA's job—the job of selling cheap power to people who want it. And having noted this, we should pause for a moment before the part of the canvas that depicts the Electric Home and Farm Authority promoting and financing the sale of low-cost electrical gadgets; before the towns of Tupelo and Athens, which, as customers of TVA, are buying more than twice as much power as before for less than half what they paid before. And before the farmers of Alcorn County and the citizens of Corinth who, combined in one association—which may well be model to the whole future of rural electrification—are buying power at one low and level price, and through membership fees and revenues are acquiring, from TVA, their transmission equipment. And before the farmers of Lauderdale County, TVA customers who are nicely giving the lie to the journalist who, last fall, snapshot every poverty-stricken privy he could find and laughed at the possibility of such farmers having power-buying power. And before those fourteen municipalities of Northern Alabama for whose use TVA contracted, with Alabama Power Co., to buy transmission equipment. And before the Birmingham court where certain preferred stockholders of A.P.C. protested that sale and the constitutionality of the whole TVA. And before Judge W. I. Grubb, who ventured no definitive answer to the loud question of constitutionality but whose opinion—quite definite enough—was that TVA is running an illegal business. And who likewise forbade the fourteen towns to accept PWA loans with which to build their own transmission systems. And before the heavy potential customers Knoxville and Chattanooga, which are respectively building and, having voted, preparing to build, their own transmission systems. And in Washington, before Senator Norris and Representative Rankin (of Mississippi), co-sponsors of the original TVA Act, who last March were hammering through protection against further delay by litigation.

And before the three directors. They were inclined, perhaps strangely, to name Judge Grubb's decision "a TVA victory"; nevertheless, a few weeks afterward, they came in a unanimous flying wedge north and into a huddle with the President. Since that time they have been confident of a favorable settlement of that question which rests for the time being in the beard of Chief Justice Hughes—and confident too that legislation can mend what the bench may conceivably damage.

And if still you think their road is steep into dubious frontier and their whole endeavor a gamble, remember that roads which lead to high places commonly have that character; and that, for an instance, the establishment of this government was in its time a gamble. And: that if some gambles have turned out worse than that, some others may turn out better.

The New Public Power Policy

Now we may use TVA to illustrate the significance of a new public policy toward power that Mr. Roosevelt expounded prior to his election and that he has applied on a magnificent scale since his assumption of office. In 1932 he declared that "the natural hydroelectric power resources belonging to the people of the U.S. or the several states shall remain forever in their possession." Further elaborating this doctrine, he asserted that four federal projects—Boulder Dam (initiated under his predecessor), the St. Lawrence Development (since stymied by a rebellious Senate), Muscle Shoals (now assimilated by TVA), and the Columbia River (site of two huge projects) —would be used as yardsticks to measure and regulate power rates in the public interest.

Here it is instructive to observe how this initial hydro yardstick is actually being applied. First, power capacity is being constructed without reference to present or immediately anticipated demand, on the theory that low rates will ultimately build up demand sufficient to absorb it. Second, rates for the sale of TVA current have been constructed not on the basis of the present cost of the limited power sold, but on the basis of estimated costs of future energy after TVA has created the new market to take up its additional power. Third, TVA has pursued the policy of purchasing distribution systems to be turned over to municipalities contracting for TVA power. The courts have restrained the execution of some of the contracts—and it must be admitted that some of TVA's bargains were concluded under the threat that if the utility companies did not sell out the systems TVA wanted, Public Works funds would be allocated for the construction of duplicating facilities. While apparently TVA made an honest effort to pay for the properties it so acquired at a fair valuation, it is evident that it holds powerful weapons against its adversaries.

Leaving for later discussion the question as to how comfortably the power industry has adjusted itself to the new dimensions laid down for it by TVA's yardstick in the Valley, let us look for a moment at what is going on at the other federal power sites. . . . There are three things to be borne in mind in connection with these dams: it is apparently the government's intention to develop power at each of its dam sites; each such hydro project is to become a yardstick; and, judging by the TVA precedent just examined, the steps in constructing a yardstick are, first begin to build the power, then determine the rates at which it is to be sold, then wait for the desired market to develop accordingly.

Traveling westward to these other federal dam sites, you would be impressed with the thinning out of population and industry, and with the great rivers whose fugitive power is to be trapped and shot through the penstocks of the government generating plants. By the time you had reached Grand Coulee you would probably have been struck with the thought that soon the West will be teeming with new yardstick power, and with the vision of millions of federal watts, all dressed up in a new suit of rates, but with no place to go.

TVA and Adversaries

This summary review of the federal power program places a new accent upon TVA, not as a rate yardstick but as a measure of the contentious ingredients that are poured into the seething cauldron of the power issue. The utility companies assert that the new federal current that will soon be humming through the Tennessee Valley is all surplus power, and that if it is to be sold, it will not measure them but destroy them by absorbing their market. The coal operators raise the cry of mayhem, and declare that hydroelectric development in the Tennessee Valley will displace the coal that now fuels the private steam-power plants. Further, they say that each kilowatt year produced by a hydro plant will supplant six tons of coal and throw out of work six men. Their multiplications add up to disaster. To these lamentations TVA replies about as follows: you power companies don't know a good thing when you see one. Instead of taking your market, we are developing it by introducing low rates and forcing you to match them. It may hurt for the nonce, but eventually with TVA rates and education in the Valley, the housewife will cook with your power, and the farmer will call upon you for the power to pump his water, milk his cows, and refrigerate his surplus produce. Moreover, we shall bring new industry to the Tennessee Valley to utilize its many natural advantages. Before we are through, the home, farm, and factory will want to buy all the power both of us can produce. As for you coal operators, you are like the liveryman shaking his fist at the horseless carriage. You are setting your face against the march of progress. . . . You blame TVA for the loss of your market even though utility steam plants only absorb 8½ per cent of your output. But because we don't want any sick industries in this Valley, just see what we are going to do for you—something you did not have the imagination to do for yourselves. We are going to create a new market for coal in the Valley by developing metallurgical and chemical industries. Many of these industries cannot afford to operate except in the vicinity of cheap hydro power such as we shall provide, but they require immense quantities of coal or coal products. Electrothermal processes, for example, require an average of more than one-third of a pound of coal for every kilowatt of power they consume. Ammonia, for another example, is made from the distillation of coal, and this is an element essential to many of the chemical industries that we shall bring to the Valley.

So there we have TVA's answer to the No. 1 question of the power issue. It seems probable that TVA will succeed to a measure in its industrialization program, because the Valley will possess a happy combination of cheap power, cheap water-borne transportation, and the mineral and forest elements that are peculiarly important to industries requiring a relatively high ratio of electrical costs to manufactured costs. In their strategic retreat from this phase of the controversy, the coal operators raise a fierce cry of "Socialism," and the power men throw back the taunt that no private industry will be willing to move into an area of government operation: first, because public power production is likely to develop into public interference with industrial customers; second, because a business operated under the control of changing administrations and Congresses of many complexions will never have the assured stability necessary to industrial health. Another protest comes from the chambers of commerce in regions having important ceramic, metallurgical, and electrochemical industries. They complain that TVA is trying to elope with their breadwinners. And here the controversy rests.

But granting that TVA will succeed in the double-barreled program for the absorption of most of the surplus power in the Valley it rules, the question remains as to what is to become of the balance of the surplus billions which, according to our estimate, will soon be available for industrial and commerical use within transmission distance of other federal power sites. The particularly favorable mineralogical and geographical conditions in Tennessee and Alabama do not obtain in the vicinity of many of them. And the industries to which power rates are of determining importance are so limited in number and value that TVA will probably accommodate all of them and have power left over to boot. Here leading the horse to water is likely to be an even greater problem than making him drink.

📌 10. "Why Social Security?" A few angry voices protested against the enactment of the Social Security Act in 1935, but it was overwhelmingly adopted by Congress. It was a mild measure, no more than a first step toward a strong program; in subsequent years Congress increased its benefits and extended its coverage. It had been enacted partly in response to widespread public pressure, especially from the aged, but one of the serious tasks of the Social Security Board was to explain to the American people why the new program was needed and how it could help them. Part of this explanation follows. *Mary Ross,* Why Social Security? (*Washington, D.C.s Social Security Board, 1936), 11-32.*

During our lifetime it has become increasingly difficult for a family to pull together and go into business for themseves in one way or another.

For years there was good land to the westward to be had for the taking. Homesteading was an outlet for the sturdy and ambitious. In the towns, family shops and businesses were carried on with relatively small amounts of capital.

There is no more free land on which a living can be made. A farmer needs machines as well as skill and grit if he is to compete in the market. In the towns and cities, modern methods of production and merchandising have greatly increased the experience and capital needed to go into business and stay in business.

Individual enterprise, which so often meant family enterprise, now plays a minor part in earning our national income. Including the farmers, only about one in five of the gainfully occupied works for himself. As a nation, we no longer work as individuals or families, but as employees. . . .

While life became safer, the chance to earn a living became less secure. The growth of employment in basic industries began to slow up. Machines and improved methods made it possible to increase output without increasing the number of workers needed to produce it. Then, for the first time, one important field of work after another reached its peak in employment and began to decline—began to use a smaller number of workers. . . .

All [the] changes in the kinds and places and time of work have made the demand for workers changeable and uneven. As a result, many workers—especially industrial workers—were without jobs even in boom times.

The Committee on Economic Security found that in the years 1922-29 an average of 8 per cent of our industrial workers were unemployed. In the best of those years, nearly 1,500,000, on the average, were without jobs.

When hard times came, further millions lost their chance to earn a living. By 1932 and 1933 industrial unemployment had risen to about 39 per cent. That meant two industrial workers out of five—10,000,000 or more in all.

The word "unemployment" was not used in English dictionaries before 1888. "Unemployable" came into use only a year earlier.

As far as we can look back, men and women, of course, had lost one way of earning their living and had to find others. Groups of workers, like the hand weavers, had seen their work taken away by machines. But it is only recently that we have realized that there could be a widespread situation—even in good times—in which large numbers of people who needed to work and wanted to work had no chance to do so.

It was not until machines had knit our lives closely together in industry and trade that unemployment could weigh down families throughout a community or a nation. Only recently have we realized that the requirements of work have become so specialized and exacting that at any one time some people cannot hold any paid job.

In our present money economy, unemployment has become a common hazard of family life like the epidemics which swept our cities three or four generations ago. A family's livelihood can be cut off as quickly and unexpectedly as their lives once were cut off by typhus, yellow fever, or cholera.

Unemployment is like a contagion also because it spreads. When a big factory shuts down, its whole neighborhood and city suffers. The livelihood of all who have been selling their goods and services to those wage earners is affected—storekeepers, landlords, doctors, barbers, owners of movie houses, and, in turn, the workers whom they employ and those who produce the goods they sell. When large numbers of people in one part of the country are without earnings, families on farms and in cities hundreds of miles away may find their living less secure. . . .

Family Security and Social Security

The words "social security" have become popular in the last five or ten years. Actually the right and duty of a community to protect its members is as old as the records of men. Primitive tribes have rules and customs to assure the safety of all.

Even pioneer American families, of course, relied on each other for help in trouble and emergencies. Barn-raisings and corn huskings, which have lasted down to our times, are a survival of years when a household asked the neighbors' help in an emergency, knowing it would give its help when its turn came.

In the Colonies, drawing their traditions from England, a husband was obliged by law to support his wife in the manner justified by his circumstances. He was liable for the debts she had contracted before her marriage, as well as later ones. She had a right to inherit part of his estate when he died. In these ways, law and custom, as well as affection, protected the security of persons least able to get security for themselves.

Since a living was made in families, it was through families that a community made and enforced its security measures.

Many of these measures remain with us today. The security of children, wives, and aged parents does not depend upon the willingness of their relatives to support them. It is written into our laws and enforced daily in our courts. It is a form of social security because we see to it as a society that relatives give this support when they can, whether they wish to or not.

Security in Health and Safety

As cities have grown up we have taken another series of steps for social security by banding together to pay for certain kinds of protection that no one family can provide for themselves. We have police and fire departments, for example. We make fire laws governing the kinds of buildings that people may build in safety to themselves and their neighbors. We support public-health departments. We set up traffic regulations to protect safety of life on the highways and streets.

We also have taken steps to aid helpless people who need a kind of care or an amount of protection that few families can provide for themselves. As our increasing scientific knowledge showed the need and the way, we built hospitals for the mentally sick and for people with tuberculosis. We made laws and opened clinics and special schools for crippled children.

At first these measures to help unfortunate people dealt chiefly with those who were dangerous to others, such as mental patients and people sick with communicable diseases. More recently we realized that it is public economy as well as kindness to make sure that other disabled people get care, since often they can recover enough to earn a living for themselves. It is cheaper to cure them than to care for them for years in institutions. . . .

In the past forty years many states have passed laws to promote health and safety in work for adults as well as for children—laws governing hours of work, night work, dangerous work, and the like. These are conditions which workers no longer can control for themselves as they could when they worked at home.

Security of Livelihood

And in some ways we have taken steps toward assuring not only health and safety in work but also the money to which working families must look in order to buy their living. . . .

In the past twenty years many states have taken steps to give some security to another large group of their people—the old people who never will earn again. Arizona passed the first old-age pension act in 1914. After the World War one state after another rapidly followed suit. By the end of 1930 fourteen others had put such laws on their statute books, and in the next three years ten more were added.

This wave of laws to pay regular allowances to needy old people did not come by accident or imitation. It came because of the growing percentage of old people in the population and the inability of the old to work for their living. Old age was becoming an increasingly serious problem to old people and their families and their towns and counties.

Most of the allowances given to old people under state laws have been very small. Even so, they have helped many old people to stay in their own homes and to keep their self-respect when they share the homes of others. Giving allowances has been cheaper as well as more humane than caring for old people in poorhouses. . . .

In January 1932 Wisconsin passed the first American unemployment compensation law. This law is unlike those mentioned above. It does not apply to people who cannot work because they are too young or too old or too sick. Its purpose is to promote the security of the able-bodied.

Workmen's compensation acts protect workers from the costs of accidents at work. Unemployment compensation acts protect them against some of the costs of the accident of not having any job at all.

Under unemployment compensation, payrolls or wages or both are taxed in certain industries to pay workers in those industries a part of their wages for a time while they are unemployed through no wish or fault of their own. In some countries these payments are supplemented by governmental grants from general taxation.

The tax borne by employers is a charge on industry, like other costs of doing business. When workers also are taxed, their payments are like premiums paid for fire insurance or accident insurance. The many people who run a risk pay toward meeting the loss of those on whom catastrophe falls. The lucky help pay for the unlucky. It is worth their while to do so, for they do not know when catastrophe may hit themselves.

Under the systems of unemployment compensation so far established in the United States, unemployed workers still carry a large part of the loss of being without jobs. Unemployment benefits usually do not begin until a man has been out of work for several weeks. They provide only a part of the amount he would have earned. They cease after a limited period, even though he still has not found another job.

Benefits paid to unemployed workers cushion the shock of losing a job, especially in short-time unemployment, which is the most usual type of unemployment in ordinary times. They make it possible for workers to keep on buying their living while they are looking for other work. In that way, these payments also benefit all those with whom these workers ordinarily deal.

Unemployment compensation is not charity or relief but a means of preventing need for relief. Through unemployment insurance, like other types of insurance, a loss which is crushing to those who incur it in any one month or year is made bearable by being distributed over large numbers of people and over a period of time.

Saving for a Rainy Day

Our expression "saving for a rainy day" recalls the times when families stored wood in the shed and food in the cellar and pantry for seasons when it was difficult or impossible to go out to fetch them. Why do they not store money in the bank now for the time of unemployment or old age when it cannot be made?

There is an answer to that question in a study made by the Brookings Institution, which analyzes the incomes and savings of families in our richest year, 1929.

In that year, the study found, families with incomes under $1,000 spent, on the average, more than they received. They drew on past savings or got outside help or went into debt. Those families with incomes of less than $1,000 represented a fifth of all the families of the nation in 1929.

Families with incomes of $1,000 to $1,500 kept even, on the average, but saved little, especially in the cities where everything had to be bought and living costs were higher. These families represented another fifth of all the families in that year.

Thus the study found that about 40 per cent of our families saved very little, as a group, in our richest year for the hard times that were coming.

Practically all the savings of that prosperous year were made by the families at the top of the money ladder.

About 10 per cent of us had family incomes over $4,600. They were found to have made 86 per cent of all the savings.

Another 10 per cent had family incomes of $3,100 to $4,600. They were found to have made 12 per cent of all the savings.

The great majority of American families—the 80 per cent who had incomes under $3,100 in 1929—were found by that study to have saved only 2 per cent of all that families saved that year.

Could the 80 per cent have saved more than they did?

The Brookings study declared that at 1929 prices a family income of $2,000 "may perhaps be regarded as sufficient to supply only basic necessities." An income of $2,500 was "a very moderate one."

Even low-income families today are likely to regard as necessities things which their parents may have done without, such as running water, electricity, haircuts, movies, a greater variety in clothing and diet. It costs more to be sick. Medical care is better and, hence, more expensive. An employee who loses time from his job because of sickness often loses pay and sometimes loses the job as well.

But what would be the result if all families did save as much as they could by doing without all but the barest necessities?

The families who now save little—those with low and moderate incomes—make up a large share of the markets on which our living depends. In 1929, 70 per cent of all the families were under the $2,500 mark which the Brookings study defined as "moderate." The spending of that 70 per cent is necessary to hold up the fabric of trade and industry on which the living of the nation depends.

When a large part of the population cuts down spending, that fabric sags, and workers and others feel the weight of hard times. That is what happened in the early years of the depression when fear and necessity made people stop buying.

There seems no question of the willingness of American families to save when their incomes approach a comfortable level. But the evidence of this study shows that most families, and especially the families whose risks are greatest, have little to look to when a rainy day comes. Their security lies in the steadiness of their earning and the safety of what savings they are able to make for the years when they no longer can earn.

When trade and industry gathered homes into closely built-up towns and cities, it no longer was safe for each house to have its own well. The safety of the whole town made it necessary to have a town water supply.

The safety of all of us now depends also on the general streams of earning and spending. Unless many families are buying—are paying money into a common pool by their spending—the stream of earnings is lowered, and all have less chance to earn. The well-being of country families and city families depends on the ability of other families to buy.

The security of families has followed their work out of the homes. Social security no longer is homemade.

The Social Security Act of 1935

The Social Security Act of 1935 grows out of these many changes in American life. It consolidates our past experience in meeting insecurity. It also sets up a bulwark against some of the newer kinds of insecurity that threaten large numbers of us in this twentieth century.

Several parts of the Social Security Act deal with groups of people whose troubles we have recognized for many years. These provisions consider the people who are too young or too old to earn or are physically handicapped. The Act authorizes federal grants-in-aid to enable the states to broaden and extend regular allowances for needy mothers, the needy blind, and the needy aged. It authorizes grants-in-aid for state services for child welfare, for crippled children, and for physically handicapped people who can be helped to work again. The provisions for child welfare apply especially to rural areas.

These sections of the Social Security Act draw on our national resources to help all states to do better what most or all have undertaken in some way and to some degree. They give a way to put into effect the best measures we have been able to devise for helping people who are unable to help themselves.

Other provisions of the Social Security Act recognize the risks of sickness—risks which affect all of us, young and old, rich and poor.—The Act authorizes federal grants-in-aid to help states to give service for the health of mothers and children and to strengthen and extend public-health services. It authorizes funds for the study of national and interstate health problems. These parts of the Act promote security by preventing sickness and by giving children, especially country children, a fair start in life.

Finally, two provisions deal with insecurity in earning. They apply to groups of our people who have moved into occupations where earning often is risky. They cover a great share of the wage earners who are wholly dependent on their ability to buy a living.

Under one of these provisions, the Social Security Act sets up a framework to protect the states which wish to enact laws for unemployment compensation. Federal funds are authorized to help a state to do this by meeting the costs of administration.

The Social Security Act does not say that any state must have an unemployment compensation law. It does not say what kind of law a state should have. It does say that business in a state which has unemployment compensation shall not be penalized in competition with business in states which do not.

From the beginning of 1935, when the possibility of harmony in state action became clear during the discussion of the Social Security Act in Congress, and up to April 1, 1937, forty-two states and the District of Columbia had enacted unemployment compensation laws. These laws are a beginning in making the costs of industry's fluctuations a charge upon industry rather than only on the jobless workers, who hitherto have borne the brunt of industrial change.

The Act thus helps states to find ways in which workers and employers can steady livelihood. It also provides ways to build up the livelihood of wage earners in old age.

The Social Security Act establishes a system of federal old-age benefits which will provide monthly payments, in 1942 and after, to many workers when they reach the age of sixty-five. The amount of a man's benefit depends on the wages he has received in his working years, after 1936, as defined in the Act. Thus old-age benefits are based on wage records.

Under another provision of the Act, grants are made to the states for old-age assistance. Old-age assistance is not the same as old-age benefits. In old-age assistance federal, state, and local funds are used to help old people who lack means of their own. Regular assistance may be given to any aged person who is entitled to aid under a state plan approved by the Social Security Board. Thus old-age assistance is helping those who now are old and in need.

Old-age benefits, on the other hand, offer future provision for large groups of people who now are working and earning. Under the plan for old-age benefits, the majority of the nation's wage earners can look forward to a definite old-age income of their own. Their old-age benefits will supplement any savings these workers have been able to make. They do not have to prove that they are needy. The benefits are theirs regardless of need.

If a worker dies before he has received his benefits, his estate receives a lump sum equal to 3½ per cent of his wages counted toward benefits.

In general, the Social Security Act helps to assure some income to people who cannot earn and to steady the income of millions of wage earners during their working years and their old age. In one way and another taxation is spread over large groups of people to carry the cost of giving some security to those who are unfortunate or incapacitated at any one time. The Act is a foundation on which we have begun to build security as states and as a people, against the risks which families cannot meet one by one.

The colonists and frontiersmen wanted independence. They wanted a chance for themselves and their children. They wanted a place of their own and an active share in the life of their times.

There is no reason to think that our wants have changed.

These are the things that most Americans ask today. What has changed is the way we take to get them. Families no longer can carve out security for themselves. Our security is the security of a people.

✔ 11. Selling social security on the state level. The Social Security Act provided that the federal government would share with states the cost of providing for destitute aged, establishing unem-

ployment insurance, and caring for dependent mothers and children and others requiring aid. Consequently, states had to enact
requisite legislation or lose the federal aid. Gertrude Springer
describes the campaign to provide social security in one Southern
state. *Gertrude Springer, "So We Told 'em Plain Facts," Survey
(April 1937), 106-107. Reprinted by permission of Helen Hall.*

The old colored woman was making a great business of selecting
two 5-cent wash cloths, and the salesgirl obviously lacked the technique of waiting on two customers at once. Miss Bailey, curbing her
chronic Northern impatience, watched the transaction. The wash
cloths must be yellow and they must have "fancy wroppin'"—which,
translated, meant a gift package.

"Lan's, Miss Hattie, I couldn't a give no golden weddin' present
this year a year ago. I sure does 'preciate this human security."

Miss Bailey felt her ears go up like a hound dog. This was what
she had come for, and she'd found it in a five-and-ten store!

Miss Hattie, proceeding leisurely with the "fancy wroppin'," took
up the topic.

"I reckon everybody appreciates it that has it, Mary. But what
you goin' to do if the legislature don't vote the money to keep it up?
That money's goin' to be hard to find."

"Yessum, Miss Hattie, but these gennlemen ain't goin' to turn us
old folks off. They jes' kain't afford to. They'd lose all that money
from Washin'ton. An' now that all us knows all the fac's 'bout human
security, they'll jes' hafta fin' the rest o' the money. Thank yo, ma'am,
Miss Hattie, that's sure a nice lookin' golden weddin' present."

The old woman pottered off and the salesgirl turned to Miss Bailey,
now more anxious for conversation than to make her small purchase.

"Did she mean that she has an old age allowance, and how did she
come to know so much about it?"

Miss Hattie straightened her counter as she answered.

"Yes ma'am, that's it, only we call it human security here and we all
know about it. We learned about it because we were going to vote
about it. After our human security week you'd 'a' had to be deaf,
dumb an' blind not to know. I reckon Mary's right; now that we all
know the facts the legislature just can't rightly afford not to find the
money."

Miss Bailey took that thought with her out into the sunny park.
Settled on a bench beside a flaming hibiscus she turned it over in her
mind. That the legislature would act—couldn't rightly afford not to—
because we, the people, know the facts. Whew, that was something
for the book! She had heard that a particularly strenuous campaign

for social security measures had gone on in this reputedly "backward" state, but, being slightly case-hardened in such matters as "weeks," had not given it too much importance. But that the facts should have penetrated to the old Marys and Miss Hatties of this easy-going little town, and along with the facts an awareness of what moves legislators to action—that was something different again. She had to know more about "our human security week."

They were forthright about it in the office of the state welfare department, spearhead of the campaign. There had to be an amendment to the state constitution before the terms of the federal Social Security Act could be met, indeed the existence of the state department itself, scraping along precariously on left-over FERA funds, probably was at stake. Nothing could happen without the amendment authorizing the state to appropriate money for public assistance purposes. "And so we put our backs into it."

While a girl was spreading out the record of the amendment campaign, Miss Bailey heard something of the events that had preceded it. Prior to FERA there had been little or no history of relief in this sun-drenched state. Life was simple and easy. Anyone with a hoe and a fishing pole was fairly certain not to starve. There were poor-farms for the old, the county "pauper lists" for the destitute. "And I don't mean the kind of destitute you no'th'nahs mean, I mean honest-to-God destitute. There's a difference."

But the depression, on top of a collapsed boom and a couple of first-class hurricanes, changed all that. There was too much honest-to-God destitution; the old simple ways could not cope with it. Then came the FERA, greeted at first almost as an answer to prayer; later criticized for "ridin' a high horse . . . and what's goin' to happen when the federal folks pull out?"

The federal folks had thought of that too, so they welcomed—some said they instigated—the action of the legislature in setting up a well blue-printed state welfare department even though it hadn't a thin dime to bless itself with, and couldn't have until the state constitution was amended. The FERA found some money it could allocate for administration, and organization got under way. There was a strong state staff reaching out to district boards and staffs which in turn reached into the counties. Although there was little or no money for relief the new organization found plenty to do; much that had long needed doing.

At its 1935 session the legislature proposed an amendment to be submitted to the electorate which would permit the state to provide for "a uniform state-wide system" of public benefits "and appropriate

money therefor." It was a first step but there was a real possibility—
such was public inertia—that it might be the last. Only if the amendment were carried with a whacking big majority at the 1936 election
would timorous legislators be moved to further action.

"If we could only make a beginning on old age assistance, only have
something to show," said the state welfare folk, and the district boards
and staffs. There was only one possibility, so remote that no one
really believed it could be realized. The state could not vote funds to
meet federal old age grants. The counties could, if they would, vote
"poor funds" for that purpose if they had any funds. But if the state
could collect from the counties would the Social Security Board blink
at its rules and match the lump sum?

The Social Security Board was not very warm to the idea but
finally agreed to it as a "temporary emergency" due to expire after
the next legislative session. Then began a great scurrying around to
bring in the counties. It was not easy, for some of the counties were as
broke as the boom, and not a dollar would Washington lay down until
every last county had made its contribution. Each county was promised
that every eligible poorfarm inmate and "county case" would be given
first preference for old age assistance. Each county needed not only
to put up more than it was now spending on its aged, but must put it
up quarterly in a lump sum, to be sure it got its money back doubled
with federal money. The same percentage of needy in each county
must be taken care of, the program must be on a uniform statewide
basis and the accident of which side of a county line you lived on
could not make the difference in getting or not getting assistance. It
took a good many months, a lot of persuasive argument by district
board members and strong appeals to local pride—"what will the rest
of the state think of us if we block everything"—before the last
doubtful county commissioners "found the money."

The upshot was that for a good month or so before the election the
welfare people had "something to show." The allowances were not
large, at least they would not seem so to "no'th'n" eyes, but they were
large enough to get a good many old folk out of the poorfarms and off
the "pauper lists." So effective was the demonstration that more than
one harassed board of county commissioners asked the district boards
and staffs to take over and manage their "pauper lists" and relief
money. "Our politicians think that relief is just a headache. 'Relievers'
don't pay the poll tax and can't vote."

But even with "something to show" there was still so much indifference to the amendment that something had to be done if it were to be
carried with the force of a mandate. "And so we decided to put on a

good old-fashioned drive. We called it Human Security Week. That sounded a little community chesty, but it said what we wanted it to say."

There was not much new or strikingly original in the plan of the campaign as Miss Bailey looked over the record spread out for her. On paper it was like most of the big drives for what Bostonians call "divers worthy causes." There was an imposing statewide committee of prominent citizens, a governor's proclamation, a speakers' bureau, posters, leaflets, car stickers, radio programs, and a spate of newspaper releases, their acceptability evidenced by a great fat clipping book.

It was only when Miss Bailey really dug into all this material that she began to see why this campaign had been different, why the "facts" had penetrated so far.

It was a fact campaign broken down to meet, within the area of its own experience, every community and every organized force in the state. It did not harp very much on the human sympathy appeal but took human decency for granted and went on from there. It made little or no attempt to put forward a social philosophy or to "educate the public." That could come later; the issue here and now was to roll up a good majority for the amendment. Since fear of increased public spending and taxation was uppermost in the public mind, the campaign managers—in effect the staff of the state welfare department—rode full tilt at the dragon of dollars and cents. The federal-state plan of financial cooperation, made possible by the amendment, would relieve counties of a large part of their burden for dependency. "Look what it has already done about the aged; it has made $2 grow where only a dollar grew before. More old folks are being cared for and better cared for, even if the counties are spending a little more than before." The point was constantly driven in that unless the amendment was passed, thereby enabling the legislature to act, the state would actually lose money. "Here we have a chance to get back from the national government a part of what our citizens pay in income and other federal taxes. . . . As a state we are now getting so-and-so much for our aged. Without the amendment we shall lose all that as well as the possibility of assistance for our children and our blind people. We can't afford to lose this money."

Miss Bailey could see all this as effective argument for large meetings, but it did not explain old Mary and Miss Hattie. "However did you get it through to them?"

"By taking it to them where they were and giving it to them in doses of a size that they could swallow," replied the sun-browned girl who had been at the hub of the whole business. "When we asked old Mary's minister to preach a sermon on human security—and we asked every last minister in the state—we did not supply him with high-powered general social arguments. We gave him the facts as they existed for his people in his county—how many colored old folks and children and blind would get allowances if the amendment carried and the legislature acted—and we left it to him to expound them. Oh yes, we had those facts, county by county, town by town.

"In the case of the Miss Hatties our speakers went where they were, to their places of employment—a five-minute meeting before the store opened—to their club and church society meetings; wherever they gathered together we followed them, gave them the facts in their own language and passed out a little leaflet that anyone who could read could understand."

"And the backwoods country?" queried Miss Bailey.

"We didn't recognize any. We used the same method in one place as in another—facts, plain facts, localized facts, presented in the simplest possible terms. We sent to every country weekly in the state an article telling the exact condition in that county—how many aged, children and blind would be eligible, how much money the county was now spending for relief purposes, how much would come into the county if the federal-state plan became effective. And if you think they didn't eat it up take a look at that scrapbook."

"You make it sound almost too simple," commented Miss Bailey. "What was the opposition saying all this time?"

"The only articulate opposition was on straight political grounds and we didn't bother about it. We were not making a political campaign. The real opposition was ignorance and indifference. So we poured out the facts and beat the big drums."

"And then came November third and the election."

"Yes and a twelve-to-one vote for the amendment."

"So what next? There's still the legislature."

"There certainly is, and a new tax-shy governor to boot. We've kept the whole subject wide open by stimulating local pressures on the members of the legislature—it's the hometown voter they answer to, you know—and by feeding out more and more facts to the newspapers up and down the state. We're as sure as time and taxes that we'll get an appropriation for old age assistance, but the real test will come on assistance to children and the blind."

Back on her park bench Miss Bailey thought over the formula: "Facts, plain facts, localized facts, presented in the language of the listener." She knew enough about publicity methods to know that this had not been easy; but it had worked. And possibly, just possibly, she told herself, this simple, concrete formula had tapped a root for social growth which could not have been reached by the exposition of a social philosophy or by an appeal for social justice. When the old Marys and Miss Hatties knew what it was all about you were getting somewhere.

Businessmen View the New Deal

✔ **12. W. M. Kiplinger explains why businessmen fear Washington.** By the fall of 1934 large numbers of businessmen were becoming hostile toward the New Deal. W. M. Kiplinger, famous for his Washington newsletter, in enumerating and evaluating the reasons for this hostility placed much of the blame upon the more advanced New Dealers. He specifically named an economist, Rexford G. Tugwell, formerly a professor of economics at Columbia University and currently Under Secretary of Agriculture, who was a favorite target of the anti-New Deal press. *W. M. Kiplinger, "Why Business Men Fear Washington,"* Scribner's *(October 1934), 207-210. Reprinted by permission of the author.*

My daily job is to shuttle between government and business, trying to explain government to business, working primarily in the interest of business.

I spend my mornings talking to businessmen callers at my office here in Washington, listening to their troubles, suggesting courses which are in line, or not too far out of line, with government policies.

I spend my afternoons in a series of interviews with government officials, high and low. They talk frankly, not for quotation, about the whys and wherefores of their doings. They explain their intentions, their difficulties, their successes, their errors. Sometimes they complain about businessmen, and sometimes they complain about other government policies than their own.

Out of this shuttling experience, day after day, year after year, quite naturally grows understanding of the problems of both sides, and sympathy with both, and irritation with both. In this particular discussion I am purposely leaning the sympathies to the side of businessmen, in an effort to show why they fear Washington.

In talking about businessmen, let's not fix a type, for there really isn't any type. Once upon a time I thought of a businessman as one who lived on a swanky street, kept a chauffeur, and sent his daughter away to a finishing school. Now, with broader experience, I think perhaps the "typical businessman" is the man who runs the local hardware store, and who may have trouble scraping up the money to send his daughter to Cleveland to attend a school for secretaries. "Big businessmen" are more prominent, but they aren't numerous. The "average businessman" is small, with a few employees, with plenty of troubles.

Businessmen have a lot of faults and deficiencies which show up in their relations to government. They are "narrow," in the sense that they are focused on their particular interests, and that they think of their business as the *end* rather than the *means* of getting things done for the community or the nation. Most are concrete in their thinking. Many have no understanding of broad economic or social abstractions. Consequently they are apt to think that anything which interferes with their operations, their "freedom," their "liberty," is wrong.

But businessmen have plenty of merits. The main merit is that they work hard to do their jobs—the jobs which our system gave them to do. They keep the wheels turning. They make business, they make work. Their motive is to get profit for themselves or their stockholders. This is the lure to keep them live, aggressive. The profit fruit is often meager, but the chance of possible profit is enough to keep businessmen awfully busy doing things which help all of us.

Actually businessmen are our principal class of public servants, although it would shock them to be told so. The fact is that they in the aggregate control the destinies of most of us to a far greater extent than do government officials. You may like the fact or not, but you must recognize it. For this reason the treatment of businessmen by the government demands attention in the *public interest,* quite apart from the profits and private interest of any particular businessman himself.

Whether businessmen have done their jobs well, or poorly, or perhaps both, is a pertinent question, but it's too big a question to answer here.

Turning to Washington officials, you find no "average type" among them. Most have become public officials only recently. A majority are amateurs at this governing business. A minority are professional public servants or politicians.

The big idea of this new set of amateur officials is to make political power ascendant over business or economic power—perhaps temporarily, perhaps permanently. The assumption is that government, acting for *all* the people, should discipline, direct, supervise, control, regulate the course of business. (This isn't a complete or wholly accurate statement, but it gives the idea.)

Thus, a new set of officials, with a new set of ideas, are trying to drive the old machine. They think, honestly and sincerely, that they can make it run better. Perhaps they can, but while they are learning to drive, they are clashing the gears, skidding the tires, flooding the carburetor, neglecting the timing, and steering from side to side. They are the drivers, but businessmen are the skilled mechanics. Naturally these mechanics grumble at the new drivers, are puzzled at the driving.

The best way of getting down to cases is to let me tell you the stories of a few businessmen who sat across the desk from me yesterday and the day before. I omit names and twist some of the stories slightly to conceal identities.

Man A: Small paper manufacturer. Finds the industry code fixes prices. This compels him to raise his price. Finds customers dropping off, going to larger manufacturers who make better-known, better-advertised brands, and whose delivery service is prompter. Thus he fears the code and the government.

Man B: Middle-aged merchant with six children. Has a fortune of about $100,000. Wants to know whether inflation will destroy this fortune and leave his children with nothing. He's frightened over inflation.

Man C: Manufacturer who needs working capital. Says he could employ fifty more men if the banks would supply credit "as they once did." Says the bankers are afraid of inflation, won't lend him a cent for a long pull. Says the government's monetary policy is cramping him.

Man D: Retired banker. Says he has most of his money invested in short-term government obligations which pay practically nothing. Says he has withdrawn from private investments, because he's afraid.

Man E: Hardware manufacturer. Wants to know what Tugwell means when he talks about the evils of the profit system. Wants to know whether the President listens to "radicals."

Man F: Metal products manufacturer. Says he belongs to three different NRA codes. Says one compels him to do certain things, and that another specifically prohibits him from doing these things. Wants to know "What's the sense in this?"

Man G: Importer, with long-term commitments. Says he can't figure out the government's monetary policies. Consequently he is hampered in his long-term commitments. Has almost ceased importing one line in which he formerly did a good business. Says the government is "very indefinite."

Man H: Vice president of a Wisconsin bank. Says Jesse Jones scolds bankers for not lending, and bank examiners scold his bank for taking a chance on some loans. Says lots of bankers think "the government will be running the banks before long."

Man I: An automobile dealer in a Southern city. Says his business has been swell. Says agricultural benefit payments helped a lot. But wonders what will happen when they cease.

Man J: Sales manager. Wants to know whether the government is going to curtail advertising eventually, as an "economic waste."

Man K: New England manufacturer. Has the jitters over the new tariff bargaining policy. Can't understand why the government fusses around about tariff just now, "when we already have about all the troubles we can manage." Can't understand the secrecy of the tariff procedure.

Man L: Small town merchant. Says farmer customers complain his prices have gone up more than their prices. Says NRA is responsible.

Man M: Large employer. Is threatened with a strike. Says the government may not know that it is fomenting strikes, but the thing works out this way.

More businessmen write letters to Washington than visit Washington.

Recently I asked my regular weekly readers to write me frankly, confidentially, without restraint, what they thought of Washington. I received more than 2,000 enlightening letters, full of first-hand information on experiences while serving here (on codes and other things), full of second-hand observations of what their fellow businessmen were saying about Washington. About 70 per cent were sour on Washington, in varying degrees. About 20 per cent were neutral, open-minded, inclined to defer judgment of current policies. About 10 per cent were enthusiastic about the general direction of government policies. There was not much evidence of partisan bias. Comments were in the business realm, not the partisan realm.

Incoming correspondence and incoming personal visitors to Washington tell approximately the same stories.

"The indefiniteness of Washington" is a subject of complaint by three out of four businessmen. They say business itself contains enough natural hazards, and on these are now superimposed a whole new set of political hazards. The objection is not so much to any single policy by itself. The objection is rather to a hodgepodge of policies which are sometimes conflicting, which are explained in different ways by different sets of officials, and which create in business minds the impression that the government is in a great state of indefiniteness and confusion.

This confusion makes fear—not fear of any one policy, but fear that the government mechanism isn't capable of administering all the ramifications of the new order. It's a vague fear, but it is more potent than any tangible situation.

Here are typical comments: "If the government would decide what to do, adopt a course and stick to it, business wouldn't mind and would adjust itself. But the continual changing of policies and the indefiniteness of the future make it hard to run business." "There seems to be no certainty. . . ." "It's hard to have confidence in the continuity of many government policies."

The uncertainties which businessmen feel about Washington may be broken down into a few major classes:

Inflation: It isn't the *fact* of inflation which is responsible for the worries. It is, rather, the uncertainty of the *time* and the *degree* and the *nature* of it when it comes. Most businessmen have come to regard inflation as inevitable. Many don't mind it; at least they are prepared to enjoy it while it is on the upgrade for a few years. But so long as they can't foresee when it will be evident, or how fast it will go, or how far, they can't easily plan ahead. Thus they play their cards close, take no chances, fear to expand.

Taxation: It's simple arithmetic to figure that taxpayers must pay the bills for current billions of emergency expenditures. The question is, Which taxpayers? Under this administration the answering finger points pretty much in the direction of business interests. Thus higher taxes of the future will eat into profits, especially "excessive profits."

NRA: Most businessmen accept the *theory* of government regulation of private industry, but they resent many of the clumsy methods of *application.* Fine schemes thought out at the top don't work well at the bottom. Changes are made from month to month. Different treatments are accorded different lines—different principles. Enforcement of codes is not yet provided in many lines. The heavy hand, the crackdown, is mixed with laxity. Too much has been attempted in too short a time, with too little system at the top to supervise all the intricacies at the bottom.

Toward the agricultural end, the AAA, the feelings are similar to those toward NRA. There's rather general acceptance by businessmen of the principle of regulation of production, but there's distrust of the methods. There's fear that the magnitude of the problem is too great for solution by a few minds in Washington.

Labor: The government favors collective bargaining. A majority of businessmen assent in principle, but want to do it in their own ways, don't want "outside unions," which means A. F. of L. unions. The government doesn't specify "outside unions," but it insists on unions independent of the influence of employers. This naturally plays into the hands of the A. F. of L., because it is the principal organizer of unions. Thus employers are apt to think the government is "pro AFofL," and that it will not protect employers against unreasonable attitudes by unions.

Inflation, taxation, NRA, and labor, these are the four main Washington subjects about which businessmen fret. Other subjects are incidental.

The government is rapidly going into the banking business. Most businessmen don't like this in principle, but they are quite apt to like it in practice. The truth is that many of the measures of government banking have come as a result of demands by certain groups of businessmen themselves.

Tariff bargaining is causing some worry here and there, but it is not general as yet.

Government experiments in the production of electricity gives concern to utilities, but is not a subject of acute anxiety to business interests in general.

Government regulation of securities and stock exchanges is generally approved as "a step in the right direction."

Dictatorial powers vested in the President are a subject of some grumbling, but at heart most businessmen prefer the focusing of responsibility. Heretofore Congress has not been popular with business. Hereafter it is likely to gain slightly in popularity, as a check against the Executive.

The quality of official personnel of the Roosevelt administration is probably a little higher than that of preceding administrations. But the tasks assumed are so much greater that the relative lack of ability shows up. The government actually doesn't have the brains or man power it ought to have to do all these stupendous things. It does the best it can with what it has.

The troublemakers, from the business viewpoint, are the highly theoretical young reformers suddenly thrust into high positions. They mean well, they are honest, they have zeal, they have imagination, but they don't have experience. They think in terms of blueprints rather than in terms of machines. Some of these young idealists have learned —the Frankfurter group, for example. Others continue in their immaturity—the Tugwell group, for example.

The Tugwellians are heartily hated by most businessmen, partly because of their "radicalism," partly because of their tactlessness in dealing with businessmen. The Tugwellians, as judged from the business angle, constitute the administration's greatest single personnel liability.

Government publicity policies have not been helpful to businessmen. Government publicity is essentially political ballyhoo. It tends to go to extremes, to be superlative, to build up false hopes on each recovery measure which comes along. Washington news, when read in the business office, seems to have an air of the unreal, the fantastic. Businessmen have come to distrust it, or to discount it. "Just another Washington blast."

If all the views of all the businessmen could be condensed into a brief address to Washington, perhaps the address would be something like this:

We know you have a hard job. We recognize the necessity for reforms, some of which must affect us. But you are forcing reforms on us faster than we can digest them. You seem to be experimenting, without knowing what it is that you are trying to find by experimentation. We accept your general leadership in the emergency, but we find your orders vague, and we don't know just what to do. Can't you reduce your program to something a little more definite, and tell us what it is, so that we may know how to plan ahead? If you will do this, we in turn will immediately increase our business, and provide more jobs than you are providing, and end the depression more quickly than you are ending it.

But the government shows few signs of heeding the pleas of business. Consequently from month to month business sentiment is becoming more restive, more impatient, more disposed to abandon its previous timidity. The movement will come to a head some time late this year. It will have nothing to do with the elections. It will not be partisan. It will be evident in a burst of "plain speaking" from various business groups. Some people will call it a "business revolt." Almost any observer can see it coming.

Then the government will heed, will make some adjustments of policy to suit business interests, will ease out some of the theoretical officials, will take in a few practical businessmen. But it never will become a "businessman's administration."

↙ **13. Marquis Childs suggests why "They Hate Roosevelt."** Just before the 1936 election, another Washington newspaperman, Marquis Childs, suggested in a vein far less sympathetic than W. M. Kiplinger why many of the nation's wealthy people and some of the most prosperous businessmen were virulent in their hatred of the President. Childs's analysis and some of his examples follow. *Marquis W. Childs, "They Hate Roosevelt,"* Harper's *(May 1936), 634-642. Reprinted by permission of the author.*

A resident of Park Avenue in New York City was sentenced not long ago to a term of imprisonment for threatening violence to the person of President Roosevelt. This episode, with the conclusions as to the man's probable sanity, was recorded at length on the front pages of the newspapers of the land. In itself it was unimportant. Cranks with wild ideas are always to be found here and there in any large community. Yet it was significant as a dramatically extreme manifestation of one of the most extraordinary phenomena of our day, a phenomenon which social historians in the future will very likely record with perplexity if not with astonishment: the fanatical hatred of the President which today obsesses thousands of men and women among the American upper class.

No other word than hatred will do. It is a passion, a fury, that is wholly unreasoning. Here is no mere political opposition, no mere violent disagreement over financial policies, no mere distrust of a national leader who to these men and women appears to be a demagogue. Opposition, disagreement, distrust, however strong are quite legitimate and defensible, whether or not one agrees that they are warranted. But the phenomenon to which I refer goes far beyond objection to policies or programs. It is a consuming personal hatred of President Roosevelt and, to an almost equal degree, of Mrs. Roosevelt.

It permeates, in greater or less degree, the whole upper stratum of American society. It has become with many persons an *idée fixe*. One encounters it over and over again in clubs, even in purely social clubs, in locker and card rooms. At luncheon parties, over dinner tables, it is an incessant theme. And frequently in conversation it takes a violent and unlawful form, the expression of desires and wishes that can be explained only, it would seem, in terms of abnormal psychology.

In history this hatred may well go down as the major irony of our time. For the extraordinary fact is that whereas the fanatic who went to prison had lost his fortune and, therefore, had a direct grievance, the majority of those who rail against the President have to a large extent had their incomes restored and their bank balances replenished since the low point of March 1933.

That is what makes the phenomenon so incredible. It is difficult to find a rational cause for this hatred. I do not mean, of course, that it is difficult to find a rational cause for criticism, even passionately strong criticism, of the New Deal. One may quite reasonably be convinced that its policies are unsound, that its leaders are hypocritical, that its total influence is pernicious. But the venom to which I refer is of a sort seldom found among men and women who have not been personally hurt, and badly hurt, by those whom they excoriate.

Some members of this class have undoubted grounds for feeling personally hurt. Some, for example, have found themselves with income still depleted, and have warrant for attributing the still sorry state of their investments to various measures sponsored by the administration. Yet others have prospered exceedingly since March 1933; and certainly on the average they find their present circumstances much improved.

As the New Dealers themselves have been at pains to point out, taxes on the rich have not been materially increased. Secretary Ickes, speaking before the Union League Club in Chicago recently, developed this at length, showing that a man with a net income annually of $50,000 would pay no more to the federal government in taxes this year than he paid last year; with $60,000 annually he would pay $90 additional; with $80,000 he would pay $775 more, and on an income of $1,000,000, an added $1,875. And although a new tax program is being drafted as this is written, probably no small proportion of the burden will be placed upon the mass of consumers through processing or excise taxes.

Surely the explanation does not lie in the trifling changes made thus far. Nor would the fear of inflation seem to account for it. In the first place, the rise in prices from 1933 to date has, by and large, helped these people more than it has hurt them. Witness the long advance in the stock market, which has doubled, tripled, or quadrupled the prices of stocks—and indeed has multiplied some of them by ten. In the second place, there is no denying that, conversely, the deflation of 1929-1933 did great damage to the fortunes of the rich. In the third place, fears of the future possibilities of the credit-inflation policy of the Administration, whether justified or not, are at any rate not fears of immediate or definitely predictable trouble. Finally—and still more important—the rich are seldom the victims of inflation. It is well known that most of the very wealthy profited from the German inflation. Long before the storm breaks, large investments have been safeguarded by diversification in real property or in stocks adapted by their nature to adjust to swiftly changing price levels. Many wealthy persons have already begun to shift their holdings to such things as farm land.

That there is a widespread conviction among the wealthy that they are being butchered to make a Roman holiday for the less fortunate is undeniable. But it is certain that as a class the wealthy have suffered relatively less than any other from the economic events of the past three years; and in that single word *relatively* there is a world of meaning. As for their feeling that butchery has at least been intended by the Roosevelt Administration, let us glance for a moment at some opinions from the other side of the fence.

A great many liberals, and certainly all radicals, complain that President Roosevelt's chief mission has been to save the fortunes of the very rich. Economists for the American Federation of Labor estimated in the annual report for 1935 that in the course of that year corporate profits—dividends and so forth—had increased 40 per cent, while real wages had increased slightly less than 2 per cent. What is more, the wage increase had been in part offset by a corresponding increase in the workweek of an hour and a half.

Surveying the present state of the nation—stock-market boom, crowded Florida resorts, thronged night clubs, the revival of luxury spending—one might almost imagine the fury of the rich to be part of a subtle plot to return Mr. Roosevelt to office. For surely such uncritical vituperation, such blind hostility, must contribute to that end. Is that it then? To throw the workers and the farmers off their guard, the American rich are simulating this rage against the man who—if one listens to the other side—has been their savior?

But such choler could not be simulated. Anyone who has seen it now and then at close range must be aware that it is too authentic for that.

While this phenomenon has gone virtually unrecorded, it is familiar to most middle-class people today. Indeed, it has had its influence upon the middle class. There are those who have been only too eager to pick up crumbs of emotion dropped from the rich man's table. In general, however, the violence of the hatred varies directly with the affluence of the social group. The larger the house, the more numerous the servants, the more resplendent the linen and silver, the more scathing is likely to be the indictment of the President. . . .

Let me turn to [a] characteristic scene. This one is in Florida. James Hamilton is the head of a firm of commodity brokers in Chicago. During the Roosevelt Administration the Hamilton firm has made a handsome profit handling various products for the Commodities Credit Corporation. And in other indirect ways Hamilton has profited from the great increase in governmental activity. He owns a considerable block of stock, inherited from his grandfather, in a flour milling company, and into the treasury of this closely owned firm the Supreme Court dumped a sum in impounded processing taxes greater than the net profits for 1928 and 1929.

But even the warm sun of Florida cannot moderate one degree James Hamilton's grim antipathy to the President and his every word and deed. At Miami Beach he sits on the porch of the cabana he has leased at one of the best beach clubs and vituperates. The President has deliberately tried to destroy the foreign market for our cotton, to the profit of Brazil. One may talk in vain about the decline in soil fertility in the cotton states, about the world movement toward national self-sufficiency, about trends and tendencies existing long before Mr. Roosevelt came into office. It is breath wasted. The President, says James Hamilton, is ruining the farmers of the Middle West by permitting the importation of corn. He will not hear you if you point out the exact number of bushels of corn that have been imported, a negligible number, or the fact that it is in considerable part corn unsuited for feeding to cattle, not to mention the graph that shows clearly how the farmers' purchasing power has mounted.

With James Hamilton is his son, James Hamilton III, also a partner in the firm. The younger Hamilton specializes in Roosevelt horror stories. He repeats with a knowing air, as having come from the inner councils, all the preposterous canards that have passed through the country by word of mouth during the past year. Many of these are built round the report that the President is insane. A number of versions of this story have become familiar. The commonest one has to do with the strange laughter with which the President greets his visitors, a laughter that—if one were to believe the story—continues foolishly and irrelevantly during most of the interview.

But James Hamilton III can improve upon these stories. He had it from a man who had dinner in the White House last week that . . . James Hamilton III becomes unprintable. He reveals with a kind of painstaking delight the horrible details of the intimate life of the first family of the land. And when this phase of the career of the Roosevelts has been exhausted, he will describe radical plots to undermine the Constitution, the church, and the state in all of which President Roosevelt has had a part.

This is not idle talk. It is for James Hamilton III the gospel, and only slightly less so for his father, who occasionally puts in a word of moderation by way of restraining young hotheads. The elder Hamilton wouldn't, in short, go so far as to say the President is insane now, but he might have been in 1933 when he seized power. For authority for the radical plots in which Mr. Roosevelt has had a hand, James Hamilton III will quote from a Hearst editorial article, from a speech by Governor Talmadge, or from any one of a half dozen weekly papers and pamphlet services that are feeding the fiercer anti-Roosevelt fires.

The social historian would do well to make a collection of these obscure papers and pamphlets, for they will one day be invaluable source material. Perhaps the noisiest of these sheets, and therefore the one that is most frequently passed about, is *The Awakener,* which is "For The Americanization Of The Right" and "Against The Socialism Of The Left." Its tone is not unlike that of the Communist *New Masses* prior to the shift in Communist policy toward cooperation with other social and economic groups, the united front. *The Awakener* goes in for headlines such as "Mrs. Roosevelt Approves Communist Youth Group." It delights in quoting George Bernard Shaw to prove that Mr. Roosevelt is a Communist. And having done this to his complete satisfaction, the columnist for *The Awakener* adds the following:

"Embarrassing item number two came to light during an investigation into the death of Joseph Shoemaker at Tampa, Florida, some weeks ago. Shoemaker, an avowed radical, and a group of friends, all members of the Workers Alliance, a Socialist organization, were busily engaged in two collateral endeavors. On the one hand they were organizing in the political field as 'Modern Democrats' while at the same time carrying on subversive agitation among the unemployed. A group of patriotic citizens resented their trouble-making activities and one night, unfortunately, they were set upon by vigilantes and flogged. Subsequently Shoemaker developed blood poisoning and died. At the time not even the most rabid anti-New Dealer offered to suggest that these 'reds,' in organizing the 'Modern Democrats,' had Franklin D. Roosevelt as an inspiration. A tell-tale letter, however, dated April 28, 1932, and bearing F.D.R.'s signature, found recently among Shoemaker's effects, brands the President as being in thorough accord with basic Socialistic principles. . . ."

This is enough to indicate the nature of *The Awakener*. And while it decants a stronger wine than the others, they all have a family resemblance. There has been a small boom in the business of issuing anti-Roosevelt publications. Although some are run for profit, others have financial backers proud to pay not only the printing bill but the cost of distribution too. "Confidential" news services that go out of Washington into Wall Street have recognized the value of the hate-Roosevelt theme.

We change the scene again—to New York. Joshua and Ellen Thornberry are giving a large cocktail party in their apartment in the east 'Sixties. The three floors of the Thornberry apartment are filled with things, things, things, a superfluity of things—a collection of jade, a collection of Persian enamels, enough Georgian silver to furnish a museum. The Thornberrys are about to leave for South Carolina for some shooting. Their large living room is filled with talk, cigarette smoke, expensive scent, and servants passing champagne cocktails. In one corner Joshua is telling three or four of his friends of a deal he had in the stock market last week that netted a neat profit. He is relating the story only to illustrate the awful kind of government we live under, with "that man" in Washington. "Why, just think of it," says Joshua, "I shall have to give 60 per cent of my profit to the government. Just think of that! That's the kind of system we live under." . . .

What one returns to—the incredible, the amazing fact—is that most of these people seem to have no realization whatever of the present plight of the world. The events that occurred between the autumn of 1929 and the spring of 1933 have apparently left no mark upon their memories. The fact that there are in the United States still some twelve million unemployed is seemingly without significance to them. The fact that when Mrs. Skeane dismissed her gardeners and chauffeurs in 1933 the dismissal was more disastrous to them than to her does not lodge in her mind. The fact that in a time when millions are destitute through no fault of their own James Hamilton is very fortunate to have a cabana on the warm sands of Florida has not dawned upon him. Nor does it seem to have occurred to Joshua

Thornberry that the plight of hundreds of thousands of families in his own city, who without governmental relief would speedily starve or freeze to death in the zero weather from which he can so readily flee, may have some logical connection with the taxing of the money which he has cleaned up in a quick and easy stock-market deal.

If you were so rude as to remind Mr. Thornberry of this connection he simply would not believe that it was real. He thinks that most of the present unemployed could find jobs if they tried, and that the rest would quickly find them if he and his like were permitted to do just as they pleased with their takings. He thinks—while he sips his champagne cocktail and looks forward to his leisure hours in the South—that the unemployed are wasters living lavishly on funds expropriated from the hard-working and the thrifty. (As he talks, through one's mind run the words of the Ghost in *A Christmas Carol* —"Oh God! to hear the Insect on the leaf pronouncing on the too much life among his hungry brothers in the dust!") Not that Mr. Thornberry is not, among his peers, a good fellow, kindly and generous. He simply is not aware of the gravity of the unemployment problem, has not bothered to look into it closely. His ignorance of what goes on outside his little insulated and padded world is abysmal.

Even more disturbing is the fact that this ignorance does not shame him. He does not think of the unemployment problem as *his* problem as an American citizen. He and others of his class who share his views appear to think that they have discharged their full responsibilities when they have touched off a string of adjectives, peppered by a few sulphurous epithets. If they cannot have at Washington an administration of their own choosing, they in effect resign from the United States. They could hardly regard with greater hostility an alien government set over them by a foreign power. (One recalls that dinner of New Jersey public utility men at which a toast to the President of the United States was greeted by a roar of laughter.) The only department of the government which they regard with anything but contempt is the Supreme Court, and the reason, stripped of its idealized protective coloring, is not far to seek: the Supreme Court has recently appeared to aid their own interests. One listens despairingly at some of their gatherings for any word which will suggest a sense that the government is a continuing instrument for the benefit of all, in the direction and support of which they expect as citizens to share, regardless of the policy or the personality which for the time being is in the ascendant.

The Turbulent Second Four Years

A triumphant coalition of farmers, workers, and the underprivileged re-elected Roosevelt in 1936 by a wide margin and in a broad geographical sweep. Roosevelt received 60 per cent of the popular vote and obtained all electoral votes except those of two New England states. Regarding his victory as a mandate for still more vigorous reform, at the outset of his second administration he sought through a complicated piece of legislation to change the membership of the Supreme Court which had been invalidating key New Deal measures. The Court fight stirred public excitement to a far greater degree than any of Roosevelt's earlier proposals, and brought upon Congress thousands of bags of mail from constituents—much of it unfavorable. During the debate the Supreme Court surprisingly handed down decisions favorable to the National Labor Relations Act and Social Security. Roosevelt lost his fight to modify the Court and therewith much political prestige but was not thereafter plagued by unfavorable decisions. Much else went unfavorably in the second four years: union battles were blamed upon New Deal labor legislation; during the apparent recovery in 1937 there was still widespread unemployment; and the recovery changed before the year was out into a sharp recession remedied only by renewed heavy spending.

✔ **14. Richard Neuberger, "America Talks Court."** A young reporter in the Pacific Northwest, Richard Neuberger (who some years later became a United States Senator), at the height of the Supreme Court fight recorded much of the public discussion that he overheard. His account is remarkable in indicating how ill-informed most people seem to have been upon even this, the most hotly debated and widely discussed, domestic issue that faced the nation during the New Deal years. *Richard L. Neuberger, "America Talks Court,"* Current History *(June 1937), 33-38. Reprinted by permission.*

He came into the diner as the clattering train neared the giant Bonneville Dam on the Columbia River. The steward seated him opposite me at a table for two, and he ordered consommé, baked ham, and apple pie with cheese. While he was waiting for the soup, he pulled a rumpled newspaper from his pocket and began to read. My impromptu dining companion looked like the average, run-of-the-mill traveling salesman or business executive that one meets in any club car or Pullman between Cape Cod and Puget Sound.

After two or three minutes paced only by the click of the car wheels, he banged down his paper angrily on the window ledge. He took out his pencil and figured lightly on the tablecloth for another minute or so. "Good Lord!" he volunteered in a loud voice. "Our taxes are going up still more. This Supreme Court plan of Roosevelt's will cost a barrel of money. Six new Justices at $20,000 a year each—that's $120,000 right there. Then they're going to let them retire at full pay. And the same thing with all the other federal courts. It's just another scheme to spend more money—like that infernal white elephant of a dam the conductor says we're coming to a little way down the river."

This seemed a fresh and novel viewpoint on the Supreme Court problem, and I listened for more. But the next statement came from across the aisle, where a casual train acquaintance of my companion had been listening to the conversation. He was seated at a large table with his family, and he leaned over the curly head of his little boy to interject, "Yes, and that's not all. They'll have to enlarge the Supreme Court building to make room for more judges, and there goes another big chunk of money. I wouldn't be surprised if this is one of Roosevelt's stunts for spending more of the taxpayers' money and putting us on the brink of inflation."

The next comment came from a man sitting behind me, who also had been overhearing these opinions. Soon, several tables at our end of the diner were engaged in heated discussion of the Roosevelt judicial reform plan. I had been on a good many trains during the last weeks of the bitterly contested Presidential campaign of 1936, but had seen little like this—when people were so stirred and interested that they put down their knives and forks to give total strangers their political opinions.

So I started doing some overhearing myself, to learn what the electorate was saying about the judiciary debate. On trains, in hotel lobbies, at public meetings, I listened to as many conversations on the Court as I could without being an outright eavesdropper. I also put questions on the Supreme Court problem to typical representatives of numerous income and cultural groups. I was not interested in the opinions of the individuals who write learned newspaper columns or deliver flowery orations on one side or the other of the question. I wanted to find the viewpoints of the great inarticulate mass of citizens who get into the public print only when they are run down by an automobile, get married, or become the parents of quintuplets. What are the American people saying about the Supreme Court controversy? Do they understand it, or are they like my ephemeral acquaintances on the train who thought the crux of the problem was the additional expense that will be incurred.

Not long ago Oswald Garrison Villard declared that the "President's Supreme Court proposal has tremendously aroused the American people and set them, from one ocean to the other, to discussing the issues involved." Mr. Villard is completely correct that the proposal has set the people to talking. They are discussing the Supreme Court in bankers' offices in New York City, and in the general store at the crossroads in Yoncalla, Oregon. Whether they are talking about the issues involved may be determined partially by considering a few randomly-noted comments:

Youthful service-station operator: "Sure, the President ought to get rid of those old fossils. I've got an uncle who's sixty-eight and I certainly wouldn't want him running the country. We have to help him around all the time, and he's never out of the doctor's office. He lives almost all the time on broth and milk-toast. And by golly, he's younger, at that, than most of those Supreme Court judges."

Young nurse: "I didn't know whether to be for or against the President's plan until I saw a picture in a magazine showing the Supreme Court's dining room. All the judges had special dishes, different knives, and forks, and special salt and pepper shakers. That settled me. I've had enough experience with crotchety patients to know that people who insist on all sorts of special favors sometimes aren't up to standard. If those judges can't use regular silverware and dishes, then they're too finicky and peculiar to run the country."

Wife of successful business man: "I know the President has never seen those dignified old men in their majestic black robes. If he had, he could never propose such a terrible thing. When I was in Washington, my husband took me to see the Court in session. It was the most wonderful sight I ever saw. It inspired me. If someone could only persuade the President to see the Supreme Court judges in that marvelous new hall, I know he would change his mind about the situation."

Worker on a WPA project: "I think big business is slipping those justices some extra money on the side. In the paper the other day I saw a picture of one of them on his country estate. They get $20,000 a year, and that's a lot of money—but it isn't enough to keep up a big estate. Where's the rest of it coming from? I'd like to see an investigation of the bank accounts of those judges. I bet they own a lot of stock; their Wall Street decisions show that."

Old man wearing Townsend button: "The President has no respect for the aged citizens of this country. He has made a political prisoner of their champion, Dr. Townsend, and now he claims that old people are not fit to serve on the Supreme Court. Providence will punish the President for this treatment of those who are old and gray. 'The hoary head is "A crown of glory,"' says Proverbs, xvi, 31. Evil days will come upon America if this Supreme Court plan is passed."

Middle-aged clerk: "The Supreme Court has brought this upon itself. The Court had no business to turn loose that communist in Oregon, and it should never have given those Negro rapers from Scottsboro a new trial. I hope the President gets rid of those two Jews and doesn't appoint any more to the Court."

A farmer, bitterly irate over the alleged tie-up of farm produce by the longshoremen's strike: "I guess our last defense is gone, now that Roosevelt is going to take over the Supreme Court. The only thing for the real Americans to do is arm themselves to protect their homes. I'm teaching my boys to shoot straight and fast."

Elderly lady: "The founders of our country knew what they were doing when they provided for nine judges. If nine judges were enough for George Washington, they should be enough for President Roosevelt. I don't see why he needs fifteen."

Young man with union button: "I'll be for the bill if the President promises he won't appoint any more lawyers to the Court. The lawyers are the ones who have wrecked everything for the common people. If I had my way, no lawyer could be a judge, a Senator, or a Congressman."

And on and on. . . .

Not by any means were all the people I talked with as apparently confused as those whose comments I have summarized briefly. But two popular fallacies seemed to have gained considerable credence. Many opponents of the President's plan claimed that the Supreme Court always had consisted of nine members, and that this number was specified in the Constitution. These people believed that the demand for a Constitutional amendment was merely for a Constitutional amendment embodying the President's plan. One of the most prevalent opinions that I encountered among rank and file citizens who were against the judicial reform bill was that the plan had to be put into effect by a Constitutional amendment because the Constitution specifies nine judges.

On the other side of the judicial fence, I heard the frequently expressed sentiment that the Court was mean and spiteful to rule at all on New Deal measures. This faction of voters refused to believe that the Court passed only on laws brought before it in specific cases on appeal. They seemed to think that when the Court got in an arbitrary, anti-farmer mood, it swung its axe and decapitated the AAA, and when it felt belligerent toward labor, it did the same to the NRA. Many Roosevelt backers appeared to regard the Court as sort of a band of villains that followed neither rule nor procedure, and roamed the New Deal amphitheatre in search of stray laws to kill.

The Supreme Court controversy has inspired a large number of citizens to poetry. A few samples may be illuminating. Here are several stanzas from a contributor to the *Star* of West Allis, Wisconsin:

> To pack our highest Court with servile tools,
> Would be the work of maniacs or fools.
> In neither class does Franklin D. belong,
> But surely in this case he must be wrong.
>
> The people raise their voices far and wide
> Against what they declare a backward stride.

And they are right, we surely ought to pause,
Or we'll be ruled by men instead of laws.

This onslaught in rhyme did not go unchallenged. Within a few days another poetic treatise appeared in the same paper:

That with capitalist tools the courts are packed,
Who decide for wealth is a well-known fact.
Yet when we ask for a change, we are denounced as fools,
By the capitalist press, and their hireling tools.

Workers and farmers and small home-owners I know,
The A. F. of L. and the C. I. O.
All want a change, and to prove they are right,
They are opposed by the chiseler and parasite.

What questions are asked most frequently by the people who seem to have a general understanding of the Court controversy? At various public forums held throughout the country the issue has been debated by special speakers, after which the audiences have been urged to direct questions at either lecturer. Shorthand reporters have been at some of these forums to take down the interrogations voiced most frequently. Here are a few of them:

From Persons Against the Plan

1. Why didn't the President say something about this during the campaign?
2. Is President Roosevelt sure the judges he appoints will be for the New Deal, once they are on the Court? Wilson appointed Mc-Reynolds, and Coolidge appointed Stone.
3. If President Roosevelt could carry forty-six States for reelection, why can't he carry thirty-six States for a Constitutional amendment?
4. Do not the 17,000,000 people who voted against President Roosevelt have any rights?
5. Will not President Roosevelt set a precedent that may some day be followed by a dictatorial President like Huey Long?

From Persons For the Plan

1. Justice Roberts seems to have more power than the President of the United States. Who elected him to be our dictator?
2. If it is true that Jefferson and Lincoln denounced the Court, isn't it all right for President Roosevelt to do the same thing?
3. Why does the Supreme Court almost always throw out laws designed to help the little fellow?

4. There is a check on the President, and a check on Congress, but what check is there on the Supreme Court?

5. Does government mean anything when the government is rendered powerless by a Court appointed for life, or kept in bewilderment wondering on which side Justice Roberts will flop?

These are typical questions from average, ordinary citizens who comprehend the basic issues at stake. The intelligent interrogations asked most frequently at the public forums have been largely along this line. Of course, there has been more than the usual run of such queries as "Isn't it true that the President is doing this so he can appoint his oldest son to the Court?" and "Didn't John L. Lewis get the President to propose his plan just to force the judges to uphold the Wagner Act?"

An astonishing fact is the great number of people who still seem to regard the problem as one of the age of the judges. Although this feature of the controversy is as forgotten as a wisp of smoke among the leading debaters of the issue, the voters themselves remember most vividly the first impression—that created when the President intimated men past seventy were inclined to be less efficient than in earlier years. Even as late as the sensational decision day in April, when the Court ruled on five cases involving the Wagner Act, I heard people solemnly arguing whether judges over seventy were physically and mentally able to continue on the bench. On the veranda of a farmhouse in the Northwest several men almost came to blows over the effect of age on vigor and alertness.

I found the human equation active in determining the point of view many people assumed toward the Court controversy. Numerous persons reduced the issue to their own personal perspective. Thus, for example, the young service-station operator was certain the President was right, because impressed on his mind were the infirmities and ailments of his sixty-eight-year-old uncle. I met another young man who was equally certain the President was wrong. This young man had a grandfather past seventy who was still keen and active, and could play golf in the nineties. The human equation was applied to the problem in other ways. A venerable and inveterate Wet approved the President's course because he had not yet put aside his wrath of many years before, when the Court sustained the constitutionality of the Webb-Kenyon liquor act.

The general objection that I heard mentioned most often by opponents of the President was that the Court is a bulwark against hastily conceived tyrannical majorities. Among the President's adherents, the point advanced most frequently was the claim that the Court has thwarted the will of the people as expressed at the polls. But beyond these general tenets few arguments seemed to go. I found that a relatively small number of citizens appeared to understand the expressions used by both sides of the debate. For example, in his radio address attacking the President's plan Senator Glass of Virginia referred several times to the famous case of *Marbury* v. *Madison*. The next day I discussed the speech with a group of people. Very few of them understood that this case was important because it was the first time the Supreme Court had overruled Congress. A streetcar motorman who had heard Glass's address was certain that it had been James Madison who had handed down the decision in *Marbury* v. *Madison*. Among average people—clerks, truck drivers, businessmen, mechanics—I met only a small number who evidenced a knowledge of such terms as "judicial review," "interstate commerce power," "appellate jurisdiction," and "general welfare clause." Equal confusion prevailed as to the Dred Scott case. Most persons had a vague recollection of the name, having heard it mentioned in radio speeches, but relatively few knew that it had revolved around the slavery question.

The argument which seemed to be the most widely understood was Senator Norris's contention that the Court should be agreed at least seven-to-two before nullifying an act of Congress.

Opinions Everywhere

Most impressive of all was the fact that virtually everyone had an opinion on the subject. It might be a lawyer or professor who could cite dozens of cases by number, or it might be a somewhat befogged farmer in Oregon who was dead sure the President was angry at the Court because it had turned loose De Jonge, the Oregon communist— but there was no one who did not have a definite idea as to what should be done. The relatively technical details, such as judicial review and the interpretation of the general welfare clause, seemed to be generally misunderstood, but the average person appeared to realize, at least vaguely, some of the issues at stake.

Just as many voters were possibly swayed by Roosevelt's personality or Landon's square-cut countenance, so did numerous people appear to be decided on the Court question by superficialities. Some said the Court looked so fine and dignified, and others claimed it would be a shame to upset and disgrace Chief Justice Hughes because he was such a distinguished-looking man. A few contended the Court was ashamed of what it was doing and thus decided its cases in secret, and a surprisingly large number were indignant at the Court because it had just been installed in a new $11,000,000 building. Others were disturbed that the justices could retire on full pay, and several Townsendites said it was unfair to give the Supreme Court pensions of $20,000 each and other people only an infinitesimal fraction of that amount. A number of farmers, irate over the AAA decision, favored a law compelling Supreme Court justices to work a dirt farm three months out of every year. A truck driver contended if the judges could be forced to drive his truck a little while, they would never rule against labor again. A baldheaded man in the clothing business declared he was for the Supreme Court until it had upheld the Wagner Act, and then he would bet his merchandise against a red nickel that the Justices had been scared into acquiescence by John L. Lewis. A logger in a fancy-plaided flannel shirt suggested that Supreme Court judges be elected every two years, like Congressmen, and another workingman had a better idea. He favored a statute to require the President to appoint at least one bona fide farmer and one laborer among the six new justices. Several women social workers said it was time a woman was on the Court. A Legionnaire declared he was a New Dealer, but would not approve the Court plan unless the President promised not to appoint any foreign-born citizens. A longshoreman was especially irate over the Court's secret sessions to discuss cases. If Congress met in the open, why not the Court? he demanded. An attorney favored a law making it a felony to denounce the Supreme Court, and a buxom housewife felt sure President Roosevelt would agree not to run for a third term only if his successor would promise to appoint him Chief Justice of the Supreme Court. The present plan was a forerunner of such a scheme, she said.

There seemed to be an opinion for every member of the population. The exception was the clerk in the shoe store who answered, "I guess the President knows more about it than I do. That's why he's President and I'm not."

15. Why were millions still unemployed in 1937? With much of the economy back to 1929 levels by the early months of 1937, some seven to nine million Americans were still unemployed. *Fortune* made a three-month study of a sampling of the half of this number who were receiving public support. Some of the findings follow. *"Unemployment in 1937," Fortune (October 1937), 99-107, 188-188B. Copyright © 1937 by Time, Inc. Reprinted by permission of Fortune Magazine.*

The depression is over. No event marked its ending as the stock-market crash of 1929 marked its beginning; hence how long it has been over no one can ever say. But everyone is willing to admit that it has been over for some time.

Everyone, that is, but a few people who are in charge of our unemployment relief. The reason why a relief administrator will hem and haw and refuse to agree with you that the depression is over is a good one from his point of view. He will point out that we still have millions of people unemployed. And he will point to the nation's 1937 bill of $1,500,000,000 for "relief" agencies. But "relief" from what?

A cynic might well say: relief from industry's lack of interest in the unemployed. Now if the prosperity indexes in most lines of business are nearing the 1929 levels, and if there is still a great deal more unemployment than there was in 1929, there is something distinctly new in our current definition of prosperity. Part of the answer is the natural growth of the population, which accounts for much of the 1937 unemployment: industry will have to push some distance beyond 1929 levels if it is to use all available workers. But is industry to blame for present unemployment? Well, industry's business is to create goods, not jobs. Assuming that its present price policies guarantee a maximum market for goods and hence maximum employment in producing those goods, then industry is not at fault for existing unemployment.

But if industry is not at fault, what is? Is the trouble with unemployment the unemployed? Many people think so. And by and large these people are almost completely wrong. Such at any rate is the finding of the study conducted by *Fortune* to form the basis of this article. . . .

Since the villain of the piece is neither industry nor the unemployed themselves, it must be sought in the impersonal mazes of the depression, which slowly sapped the effectiveness of older men and never gave the young a chance to develop the skills that are needed today. The most dramatic news written by the recovery from the workers' standpoint is that a labor shortage exists concurrently with an unemployment problem. The shortage is in skilled labor: if skilled workers could be discovered, they would each in his turn provide jobs for one, two, or five unskilled workmen.

Such is a major conclusion to be drawn from the survey. Besides this, there are many others, all of them important.

In rapid-fire order, here are the answers to eleven basic questions that are being hotly debated everywhere by citizen and politician alike:

1. Are the reliefers bums? No.
2. Have they had much education? No.
3. Did industry fire them because they could not do their jobs? No.
4. Do they ask for too much help? No.

5. Has industry taken many of them back since 1935? Yes, almost half.

6. Is there a shortage of skilled labor? Yes.

7. Is there an abundance of unskilled labor available to industry that is not being "bid away" by WPA? Yes.

8. Are those remaining on relief "marginal men" in that they are unfit for employment by lack of skill, age, or disability? Yes.

9. Are these "marginal men" unemployable? The unskilled, no; the aged and disabled, probably yes.

10. Is the WPA "spoiling" them and wasting the taxpayers' money? No.

11. Are the local communities doing as good a job of giving direct relief to these unemployables as the federal government did two years ago? No. . . .

Now for the documented answers to our categorical questions:

1. *Are the reliefers bums?* A good many U.S. citizens are absolutely certain they are. If you travel around the country you will hear people say that "by 1935 there was nothing left on relief but a bunch of worthless loafers that wouldn't take a job if you sent the sheriff to give it to them." These same people have ideas about the proper handling of the loafers. "Anybody who is on relief," they say, "should not be allowed to vote." Or, "Anybody now on relief ought to be sterilized and colonized."

The cold percentage tables . . . absolutely controvert the people who deliver themselves of such sweeping obiter dicta. More than two-thirds of our sample of the 1935 reliefers held their longest jobs for more than five years. A fifth of the total sample had held the same job for twenty years and more before hard times caused employers to let them go. A quarter of the total worked at one job for from ten to twenty years. And a fifth were good enough workmen to keep the same job for from five to ten years. This is an employment record that argues a good deal for the steady-going habits of those who were thrown out of work by depression. Moreover, of the entire sample, less than a tenth had lost their jobs through personal failure in their own business or through being fired for their own clearly apparent fault.

Sometimes the criticism of relief as caring for a bunch of loafers takes the form of yelling about the high percentage of "foreigners" on the rolls. The implication is that aliens are no-account people who don't deserve a helping hand. Even some of the reliefers themselves repeat this argument. A U.S. citizen in Thomaston, with an Irish name, complains that WPA is not fairly run because he, "a real American" with five children to put through school, was drawing the same salary as the Poles on the job. The Poles, he says, are drunks. As a matter of fact . . . the people in the sample are not predominantly "foreigners"; the aliens among them are represented in practically the same proportion that they bear to the total population of the country. Negroes did constitute 22 per cent of the sample, as compared to 15 per cent of U.S. gainful workers and 10 per cent of the total U.S. population. But here is a place where the present survey may easily prove fallible because of the heavy representation of Southern or border communities among the eleven places chosen for study.

2. *Have the reliefers had much education?* Not by any formal standards. The majority of the sample left school either before or at graduation from grammar school. Ten per cent had no education whatsoever. A fifth left school before finishing the fifth grade; another fifth before finishing eighth grade. Still a third fifth quit with a grade-school diploma. Fifteen per cent had "some high school," while only a handful had finished high school or college.

This education record is slightly lower than the government figures for education among reliefers in the U.S. as a whole. Again allowance must be made for heavy representation of Southern communities in the sample: Negroes and so-called poor white trash have had less of a chance at schooling than "the submerged tenth" or the "underprivileged third" in the whole nation. But the generalization remains the same: the great majority of the people who constituted the relief burden in 1935 had not had much education. The statistical tables show that the age categories in our sample run much higher than comparable ages for the entire U.S. population. This has a bearing on the question of education among reliefers: old people, who were at school age when there weren't so many schools in the U.S., would quite naturally tend to have less schooling than those who have come of age since the twentieth century began.

As a natural reflex of their own meager education the majority of the sample want their sons to be self-supporting at seventeen to eighteen years of age—which would indicate by indirection that they want their sons to finish high school. But the age thought desirable for self-support to begin differs with regions. In Shamokin, where book learning hasn't got much to do with anthracite mining, a high proportion of reliefers want their sons self-supporting at thirteen to sixteen. In New England Thomaston, most parents think seventeen to eighteen is a good age. In San Francisco a larger proportion of reliefers show a preference for the age of nineteen to twenty-one—proving, as one might logically expect, that a commercial metropolis tends to think in terms of more schooling or more training.

3. *Did industry fire the reliefers because they could not do their jobs?* No. This question is partially answered by the "duration of longest job" statistics cited to show that the reliefers aren't bums. But more completely relevant to it are the 1937 ratings for employability of the 1935 social burden. . . .

Of the entire sample, 45 per cent were judged to be definitely employable, 30 per cent were rated as borderline, and 25 per cent were listed as unemployable. This was in large measure industry's own decision. In other words, the men who do the employing agreed that only 25 per cent of the sample were entirely useless. Of this unemployable classification, one half were more than sixty-five years old, a total of four-fifths were over fifty-five, while 93 per cent were judged unemployable because of age or bad health or physical disability of some kind. That leaves a mere 7 per cent in the "bad attitude" class. . . .

4. *Do the reliefers ask for too much help?* No. This question is extremely controversial, and the answer a person gives is bound to be influenced by his social philosophy. In conducting its survey *Fortune* ran across a Farmer-Labor liberal in Minnesota who thought all bankers should be shot and all the unemployed liquidated by starvation; his idea was that the world belonged solely to the gainfully employed worker. But such tooth-and-claw liberalism is not common; nor is the same attitude common on the Tory side. Most people would give the unemployed something, if only a pittance from private charity. For our purposes we may adopt for a norm the government weekly-budget figure of $24.24 for a city family of four (food $8.63, rent $4.27, clothing $3.05, fuel and light $1.48, and sundries $6.81). A man on relief might naturally be expected to want at least what the government thinks is adequate for him and his family.

Actually, such is not the fact. One half of the sample cases that consist of four to a family say they could live comfortably on $22.50 weekly or less. In the South the chosen comfort standards of the reliefers run appallingly low by comparison with the government averaged budgets even for rural areas. Fifteen per cent of those in the Adams County sample think $5 to $7.50 a week would be a fine income for a family of two. Ten per cent of those in Beaumont are of the same opinion. The desires of the sample for the country as a whole run only slightly ahead of what they are getting now. For instance, a majority of those that are now getting a weekly income of from $10 to $15 either from private employment or through relief consider that

$22.50 or less is a comfortable living wage. And half of that majority would be satisfied to have an income of $12.50 to $17.50 a week. Only two-thirds of the 1935 reliefers have electricity, less than a half have a radio, under a fifth have automobiles (mostly of a pre-1930 model), and less than a tenth have telephones. Two-fifths have vegetable gardens, but oddly enough the number of reliefers in the rural South that have vegetable gardens is proportionately very low. Only one-third of the reliefers have bathrooms.

5. *Has industry taken back as many as half of the reliefers?* The actual figure is 45 per cent. Almost a half of those that have been re-hired are in the skilled and semiskilled categories.

6. *Is there a shortage of skilled labor?* Yes. Except in the depressed industries, practically all skilled labor has been re-employed. In most of the industrial regions of the sample, industry would take more skilled men from the relief rolls if it could find them. If you argue that some workers left on WPA are skilled workers, you will meet with the counterargument that they are too old. The old, according to industry, cease to be skilled when they slow down to a certain point.

To dramatize the acute hunger for skilled labor that exists in the U.S. today, let us take a brief, highly syncopated swing around the circuit of the eleven communities studied in the survey. Since the brass-goods industry in Connecticut's Naugatuck valley demands a high percentage of skills, the logical place for our trip to begin is Thomaston. In Thomaston there are two industries: the Plume & Atwood Manufacturing Co. which makes brass goods, and the Seth Thomas Clock Co., now a division of General Time Instruments Corp. During the depression Plume & Atwood, although it dropped wages to a low of 40 cents an hour for a twenty-four-hour week, laid no one off; it thus held on to its skilled-labor supply, paying wages (as well as dividends to stockholders) out of the surplus rolled up in good times. ("That's what we conceived cash surpluses to be for," says Vice President S. K. Plume.)

The Seth Thomas Co., however, had a different idea. No longer owned by the founding family, and considered by its new owners as part of a system that must show a profit "or else—" it laid people off whenever it didn't have work for them to do. Moreover, it discontinued its pension system, allowing employees who had worked for it as long as forty years to go on relief.

When the depression lifted, Plume & Atwood, needing some new men, skimmed the cream of WPA. Seth Thomas, which pays lower wages, took the remaining good men. But there were some they couldn't take: the less desirable young who knew nothing about factory work (neither company had trained any *new* skilled men for a number of years) and the old. Although Seth Thomas is at the moment concentrating on hiring men in the upper age brackets to "sort of season up the group as a whole," it does not feel that it can afford to hire too many slow elderly people or inefficient young people. "No employer," says the Seth Thomas personnel head, "can be expected to take on a contingent pension liability which is going to mature five years after he takes it on." And no employer, so the personnel head also feels, can be expected to take on the inefficient among the young if he doesn't feel free to fire them when economy makes it necessary.

The Seth Thomas and Plume & Atwood attitudes explain why the old, the disabled, and the inexperienced young remain on the Thomaston relief rolls in 1937. Seth Thomas doesn't want them; Plume & Atwood, which hung on to its skilled-labor supply by supporting it in the lean years, doesn't need them. . . .

7. *Is there an abundance of unskilled labor available to industry that is not being "bid away" by WPA?* Yes. The testimony of industry after industry, in all of the urban communities visited by *Fortune,* is that it doesn't have to go to WPA or relief for men; unskilled labor is to be had merely by wagging a come-hither finger at the factor gates. In Beaumont, Kewanee, Flint, Thomaston, and elsewhere there is plenty of available common labor that is not on the relief rolls or on WPA; it is simply a floating supply from the section of the unemployed that does not apply for relief. This floating supply naturally competes with the supply that is still available on the relief rolls or on WPA. . . .

10. *Is the WPA "spoiling them" and wasting the taxpayers' money?* People who are rabidly against the New Deal are certain that it has spoiled them. You will hear it said frequently that "employers can't get labor because they have too easy a time on the WPA and won't leave to take an honest job." You will hear housewives complain that "Since this foolish relief business commenced I have to pay $4 a week for a maid." You will hear farmers grumbling about the lack of good men to do their cherry picking, and heads of families yelling about the disappearance of the handy man who used to cut the lawn once a week.

The popular sentiment about WPA may be measured by the gags now passing from mouth to mouth. "I hear Harry Hopkins is planning to equip all of his WPA workers with rubber-handled shovels." Or: "Don't shoot our still life; it may be a WPA worker at work." Or: "There's a new cure for cancer, but they can't get any of it. It's sweat from a WPA worker."

But the people who criticize WPA fail to take into consideration certain fundamental facts. The cream of the crop who were on WPA in 1935 have been absorbed by private employment; and the very fact of their absorption is sufficient proof that WPA has not spoiled them for industry. Naturally, the men who are left on WPA tend to be older and slower workers. Where they have skills, these skills are negatived by age or physical disability. But they are not necessarily bad workers or lazy workers. To take a typical instance, in Connecticut the WPA recently completed the building of a high school in thirteen months. A private contractor would have done the job in ten. But the private contractor would have had the benefit of younger, faster laborers. Considering their age, WPA workers did a good job.

The final answer about WPA, then, would seem to be that it hasn't ruined the men who have already left its rolls, and that age and disability are what are "ruining"—i.e., slowing down—the ones that remain. Which is what one might logically expect. As for the criticism that WPA keeps farmers from getting cherry pickers and housewives from getting cheap servants, there is something to it. Men don't like to quit WPA or relief to do seasonal work that is over almost before it has begun and women on relief don't see the point of taking private jobs at what they consider less than a living wage. The classical economist thinks the government is doing something reprehensible in thus interfering with the law of supply and demand as it affects the labor market. Harry Hopkins thinks not. The issue between them will not, however, be decided on a basis of economics; it will be decided at the polls.

Sensitive to the charges of inefficiency that have been flung at them, the WPA authorities have recently ordered a "purge" of the WPA rolls. The purge has resulted in the dropping of the more inefficient of those who were left on WPA at the beginning of last summer. The ousted cases tend to fall back into the ranks of the old, the disabled, and the untrained young who are seeking straight relief. But the purge doesn't change the nature of the combined WPA-relief reserve labor pool. Industry still doesn't want many who are left on WPA—not yet, at any rate. When and if the present industrial boom goes higher, then it will absorb some of the remaining WPA workers. In a boom agricultural county, such as Scott in Minnesota, private employment has already soaked up people of a type that remains on WPA elsewhere in the country. Almost anyone is useful to agriculture if economic conditions are right. As one Scott County citizen says: "Out here in the farming country if an eighty-year-old man drops dead during harvest, they put it down to sunstroke, not old age." The real problem in boom agricultural regions is a seasonal one; in winter the lack of work hits efficient and inefficient with relative impartiality.

11. *Are the local communities doing as good a job of giving direct relief to unemployables as the federal government did two years ago?* In most cases, the answer is an unqualified negative. In some places the local community does a good job. Baltimore is one of these places. But the Baltimore local relief agencies get credit for a better job largely because the same people who ran the government relief in 1935 are still in command. They bring added experience to the problem today.

Communities like Baltimore, however, are exceptions. And in certain places, especially in the South, effective local relief is conspicuous by its absence. In Greenville, since the federal government pulled out of local direct relief, there is nothing but a Community Chest–Salvation Army appropriation of $4,000 a year, which is doled out in almost microscopic fragments to the needy. The WPA in Greenville has taken care of some of those who ought to be on direct relief but who are too proud to beg. As a result, one project of the Greenville WPA has been wholly carried out by men over sixty or certified by a doctor as unfit for work.

Adams County, Mississippi, shows local relief at its worst. Official Mississippi relief is limited to the old, the blind, dependent children, and "others." In 1936 the legislature appropriated $1,000,000 for old-age relief, and specified that it was to last twenty-seven months. This isn't enough to care for those who are over sixty-five and in need of relief; in Adams County alone there are 500 applications for help under the old-age relief law that are still waiting—and starving. Those direct reliefers in Adams County who are under sixty-five have to be satisfied with the commodity relief from the Federal Surplus Commodities Corporation—clothes made by the WPA sewing project, cracked rice, dried skimmed milk. The June allowance for this year was two sacks of dried skimmed milk and six grapefruit per relief case.

When President Roosevelt laid it down that government had a social responsibility to care for the victims of the business cycle, he set in motion an irreversible process. Every depression creates new precedents that become bench marks for the guidance of statesmen and politicians in the next. But as we have frequently implied in this article, the victims of depression divide naturally into two categories that require differing social treatment. There are those who are not permanently destroyed by time and change as potential gainful workers. And there are those who are so destroyed.

These latter make up what might be called the permanent social burden. From now on government in the U.S. will have to take care of anyone who falls into this classification. Whether it is to be the federal government or the governments of the separate forty-eight states is a question that will be bitterly fought over at the polls. And it does not matter much who does the job as long as it is done. But the point to remember is that the past depression has set up certain *national* standards for the care of the permanent social burden. States that do not at least comply with federal standards will always be the objects of invidious comparison by the less privileged—and therefore more numerous—voters. And as a matter of fact the federal government will henceforward actively help to maintain state standards at a certain level.

16. **Labor controversy and the National Labor Relations Board.** The passage early in the New Deal of the National Industrial Recovery Act with its sanction of collective bargaining had led to great unionizing drives. Under the protection of the Wagner Act (National Labor Relations Act) of 1935, two great rival efforts to organize the mass production industries got under way. Added to the labor warfare between organizers and employers was the conflict between the AFL and its new challenger, the CIO. Much that transpired not only alarmed and angered industrialists but also much of the middle-class public. *Fortune,* viewing the union drive through an analysis of the National Labor Relations Board before which many disputes were heard, not only described the Board but also gave some picture of the conflict. Part of the article follows. *"The G—— D—— Labor Board,"* Fortune *(October 1938), 52-57, 115-118, 123. Copyright 1938 by Time, Inc. Reprinted by permission of* Fortune *Magazine.*

"Great credit must be given to those employers who have led the way toward the acceptance of this law. Their calm voices have been most effective in overcoming the irrational fears which agitators have sought to cultivate. Such employers serve themselves and their country well." *Joseph Warren Madden, Chairman, NLRB.*

". . . we are addressing ourselves now to Public Enemy Number One. Fear of the inquisitorial activities of this agency [the National Labor Relations Board] has spread like a blight over management, workers, and investors of capital. The administration of the National

Labor Relations Act has been such as to snuff out the fires of industry and send millions of workers into the line of the unemployed." *Senator Edward R. Burke of Nebraska before the U.S. Chamber of Commerce, May 1938.*

"My arm will be palsied and my tongue will be silenced before I will ever compromise with a seceding movement or a common foe. . . . We will mobilize all our political and economic strength in an uncompromising fight until this Board [NLRB] is driven from power. . . . The Board is a travesty on justice." *William Green, President, American Federation of Labor, before the Massachusetts State Federation, August 1938.*

/ "The largest drawback to good industrial relations is, of course, the Wagner Act . . . He [the employer] can only be heard when he is summoned, and he knows before he goes that there is no record of a single decision where he has had a ghost of a show. So what! In the history of jurisprudence in the U.S. everyone has been equal under the law until the Wagner Act dispelled this privilege." *William S. Knudsen, President, General Motors Corp., before the U.S. Chamber of Commerce, May 1938.)*

Thus the most bitterly contested of all New Deal legislation draws its opposition from politics, organized labor, and industry. And included in this essential paradox there are other paradoxes without precedent in labor history. There is the spectacle of an American Federation of Labor president matching the indignation of a General Motors Corp. president; of a labor law condemned for its demoralizing effect on labor; of an attack on labor legislation led by employers with a record for beneficent paternalism.

Against the National Labor Relations Act (NLRA) itself its business critics return a scathing indictment. It is patently one-sided— exclusively a *labor* law. It prejudges the employer to be a scoundrel without rights in equity. It penalizes him for even a mild expression of personal opinion, but it provides no penalties for fraud, coercion, or violence on the part of a hotheaded labor minority. It sets up a Board that is at one and the same time judge, jury, and prosecutor, and provides no real opportunity for an impartial court review of the Board's decisions. The Board's findings of fact are held to be conclusive if supported by evidence—which may be interpreted to mean any evidence whatsoever. It violates the right of free speech, the rights of property, the inviolability of a contract. It promotes lawlessness, destroys discipline, and encourages strikes against society. It is in short a dangerous intrusion of radical bureaucracy into private enterprise.

Against the National Labor Relations Board (NLRB) they are no less incensed. They find it biased, incompetent, and visionary. They point to the deliberate inconsistency of Board decisions that have adversely cited the Consolidated Edison Co. of New York for *promoting* collective bargaining and adversely cited the Republic Steel Corp. for *discouraging* collective bargaining. They bring up the case of the Kentucky Firebrick Co., which was ordered to reinstate, with back pay in full, thirty strikers involved in a violent riot; the Fansteel Metallurgical Corp., which was required to reinstate, without prejudice to their seniority right, the sit-down strikers who seized its North Chicago plant and held it for more than a week against a sheriff's posse; the National Electric Products Corp., which was ordered to ignore a contract with an American Federation of Labor union and hold an election of its employees to select a proper bargaining agency (an election won by the AFofL)—and this in the face of a district-court decision that the original AFofL contract was valid and binding.

They cite an Oregon yarn-manufacturing company that was held to have violated the law because it followed the advice of the State Conciliation Board in an attempt to settle a strike; an Ohio equipment company to whose employees the Board denied all collective-bargaining privileges for six months at the request of a minority CIO union; and a North Carolina textile mill that was held to have violated the law because it *failed to protect* a union organizer from the violence of a local mob formed, in part, by its employees. Behind these seemingly illogical and inconsistent activities the average "informed observer" feels that there is a strong CIO bias, a vicious and subversive political philosophy, and a dangerous threat to the entire industrial structure of the U.S.

This point of view toward the NLRA, as most of its critics will usually admit quite frankly, is colored by emotion. But emotion is not confined to opponents of the Act. It seems to be an inevitable part of any approach to industrial relations. It is the single common denominator of such conflicting points of view as those of the paternalistic employer, the militant labor leader, the firmly entrenched president of an old-line international, the rank-and-file worker.

The result is that industrial relations have achieved the unreasoning bitterness of a holy war. They have become a battlefield of slogans and shibboleths, of coercion and propaganda, of intimidation and mutual accusation, of guerrilla warfare and strikes. It is this battlefield that the NLRB has invaded—intending, according to its sponsors, to "smooth out obstructions to the free flow of commerce"—succeeding, according to its opponents, in making an already intolerable situation infinitely worse. Drawn up on one side is an almost solid phalanx of U.S. industry led by the National Association of Manufacturers and the U.S. Chamber of Commerce, and at the moment heavily supported by the leaders of the AFofL. On the other side is the CIO and what is probably a majority of the rank and file of *organized* labor.

Now confusion characterizes this strife; and the chief reason for the confusion is the fact that two issues are almost inextricably involved. There is first the issue of whether the right of collective bargaining ought to be encouraged and protected by law. And then there is the issue of whether the National Labor Relations Act is a desirable piece of legislation and whether the National Labor Relations Board is a desirable governmental body. It is apparent that no progress can be made in clarifying the situation unless these two issues are considered in turn and separately. The man who believes—on or off the record— that unionization is a bad thing; or the man who is *against* collective bargaining by independent unions for all, or a substantial portion of, American labor—such are per se *against* the NLRA. But the antithetical position is not so clear. It is not clear because this legislation, which was designed primarily to protect a right, has become automatically (as well as by virtue of its preamble) legislation to promote and encourage a practice. Therefore those who acept the principle of collective bargaining do not necessarily agree in their attitude toward the NLRA: depending upon whether they think collective bargaining ought to be encouraged, or whether they think it should merely be accepted as a necessary and perhaps even temporary evil, they may be for the Act or against it. The latter group, which asserts itself as *for* collective bargaining in some sense, and at the same time *against* the Act and the Board, is especially important; and we shall return to it presently for a closer scrutiny. . . .

There are many ways of measuring the success of a quasi-judicial administrative agency. There is the superficial legal yardstick that measures its success by its litigation record. By this yardstick the NLRB has been phenomenally successful. Its score in the Supreme Court of the U.S. is 12 to 0; and in the circuit courts of appeal the score on September 1 stood at 34 to 14 (at least six of the Board's fourteen reverses will probably be appealed to the Supreme Court). But a far sounder yardstick—perhaps the only true yardstick—is the Board's record in making effective the declared purpose of the NLRA, which is, as already stated, to protect the right to bargain collectively. It is that record, in its strictest sense, that we are examining.

It is generally conceded that the Labor Board is the hardest working government agency in Washington. One reason is that the Board and its employees live with their jobs. Another is the sheer volume of work that has piled up since 1937 when the Supreme Court unexpectedly handed down the Jones & Laughlin decision, which convinced industry and labor that the NLRA was the law of the land.

Between October 1935, when the first NLRB hearing was held, and July 1, 1938, some 16,200 cases involving about 3,900,000 employees were brought to the Board by workers and labor organizations. More than three-quarters of these cases were officially closed during that period. Of these, about 16 per cent were dismissed by the Board or by its regional directors, approximately 25 per cent were withdrawn, and an additional 54 per cent were settled by mutual agreement. Only some 5 per cent of all the charges filed required a formal hearing before a trial examiner. . . .

Industrial warfare creates raw wounds; investigations, attempts at settlement, and hearings, are seldom carried on against a background of temperate restraint. When the NLRB moves into town it may find a situation as tense and unpredictable as a Saturday night saloon thirty seconds before the first bottle smashes the mirror behind the bar. "The s.o.b.'s think they own the town." "Let me an' him go downstairs in the cellar an' see who comes up." In a New York town the Board's attorneys were greeted with a brass band. But in Wallace, Idaho, "the goddam Communists" couldn't buy a meal. The Civil and Commerce Association of Montevideo, Minnesota, wrote: "May we offer you our full cooperation in this matter and express the hope that if we can be of assistance to you you will feel perfectly free to call on us." But during an Indiana hearing the regional attorney was poisoned twice in the same restaurant; in Steubenville, Ohio, the trial examiner was hanged in effigy; and in Newton, Iowa, Governor Nelson G. Kraschel said: "You can tell the cockeyed world that there will be no Labor Board hearings in the military district of Iowa."

This element of the unpredictable, the essentially human, carries over into the hearing room. Testimony ranges from broad farce to sheer horror. In the case of Metro-Goldwyn-Mayer Studios and the Motion Picture Producers Association, in Los Angeles in the fall of 1937, Grover Jones, veteran Hollywood writer, entertained a hilarious courtroom for two days with the raw material of a new *Once in a Lifetime*.

> Mr. Jones: They wanted eighty Indians, and I got the job only because I knew how to put on what they called bolamania, burnt umber and raw umber mixed. But they made me a chief. That meant I didn't have to go naked. I could wear a suit, you see. And at that time I was convinced I was fairly smart. So there were now eighty-one Indians. I had never seen a camera during all those months, because I was always in the background, waiting over in the back of the hill for the call to come over the hill on the horses to rescue the child.

And I had never been on horses. So we sat on these horses, each confiding in the other, and none had ever been on horses, except we were all hungry. Finally the man said, "Now look, when you hear shooting I want you all to come over the hill, and I want some of you to fall off the horses." Well, in those days they paid three dollars extra for a man who would fall off a horse because it is quite a stunt. So we waited until finally we got the call to come over the hill, and somebody shot a gun off, and eighty-one Indians fell off their horses. So I gave up acting. . . .

But in a case in Alabama, a month before, the melodrama was more authentic and considerably less funny.

A union organizer [who was testifying to an attack on union head-quarters]: About that time they were rushing the stairway . . . we put a table against the door. A portion of the glass door was exposed above the table, and bricks began to come through the glass . . . (a newspaper reporter phoned at this point). I said, "They're tearing the building down. They're tearing the offices apart and beating our men up . . . if it is possible for you, I don't know how much longer I will be able to talk, send in some state police, if you can, because, I said, I can't talk to you any longer." I threw the phone down and by that time it was my turn to run the gauntlet . . . I fell half way and rolled the rest. After I hit the street I was kicked from both sides into the gutter and a fellow was standing on top of me. I heard somebody say "That's enough, let him up." Two fellows picked me up, one had hold of each arm, and another fellow knocked me out of their arms. They were dragging me out of the crowd and one fellow was trying to choke me, had his arm around my neck, and while he was choking me a police officer did come up and say "I will take him."

From the record of another hearing comes the testimony of an employee:

Q: You had been shot?
A: Yes . . . I was under the table laying flat for ten minutes . . . I heard a man from outside say, "God, they're not blanks; they're bullets."

In North Carolina the mayor of a mill town who was also a mill employee, led a mob of 200 people to the house of a union organizer. The mayor's brother testified:

And Mr. ——— [town alderman] said "if anyone in the bunch will go with me down to [the organizer's] house I'll stick a match to the house and burn them up like rats, kids and all."

Testifying at a hearing in Michigan last year a witness described a labor riot in part as follows:

Mr. ——— [a member of the general executive board of his union] was attacked by four or five men who kicked him in the general region of his stomach and plugged him from the rear . . . and he was finally forced to the cement over to my left and there a separate individual grabbed him by each foot and by each hand, and his legs were spread apart and his body was twisted over toward the east, and then other men proceeded to kick him in the crotch and groin and left kidneys and around the head and also to gore him with their heels in the abdomen. (And later) . . . And the girls were at a loss to know apparently what to do, and then one girl near me was kicked in the stomach, and vomited at my feet. . . . I stayed there until practically all the literature had been gathered from the ground and until the girls had been pushed back on the trolley and the trolley had gone and it became very quiet around there and relatively still.

And at a hearing in New York state a strike-breaker described the aftermath of a labor riot as follows:

I met [the president of the company] in the plant about an hour or two afterwards. He had been taking pictures, moving pictures, and I really believe it was a very good stunt on [his] part because he took some nice pictures and showed how my men were showered with bricks. I believe he published some in the papers afterwards showing how the peaceful pickets molested those who wanted to go to work. In fact he identified some of these employees of his, that were on strike, throwing bricks and showering rocks on these peaceful chaps I had, wanting to go to work [a union witness described the strikebreakers as being "about the toughest bunch of men I ever laid eyes on, half of them had scars from ear to ear on their faces"]. . . . [The president] talked about the pictures. He said he had photographs about the assault and my people had done wonderful work and started to congratulate me . . . he congratulated me on the brilliant work I had done, and I said I didn't see anything brilliant about it, the men had gotten into the plant the best way they could while they were under a shower of bricks, and he was taking pictures of it. Naturally he had them published showing peaceful pickets, America, a free land, all that stuff. Naturally, it wasn't bad stuff, because those peaceful pickets were certainly raising the devil. . . .

Excerpts such as the above, lifted from millions of words of testimony, prove nothing in themselves. But they are quoted here to provide a glimpse of the background of violence, melodrama, and sheer absurdity against which industry and labor and the bright young men of the NLRB are acting out their parts in what *Fortune* last November called "one of the greatest mass movements in our history . . . comparable . . . to the great trek westward, beginning in the Mississippi Valley and ending on the Pacific Coast." And it is against this background that the Board's record and technique and judicial integrity must be judged.

With the color and the fireworks and the human element deleted, here's how the Board works in principle at least. Any employee or labor organization may go to any one of the twenty-two regional offices and file a charge of unfair labor practices. A field examiner then investigates the case, talking to the employer and employees concerned. Some 40 per cent of all cases that the Board has disposed of have been either withdrawn or dismissed at this point because of lack of evidence or foundation in fact—which helps explain why so few cases that go to a formal hearing are decided in favor of the employer. If the investigator and the regional director find substantial evidence to support the employees' contention, they usually make an effort to encourage a settlement without issuing a complaint. Among the many cases involving strikes that were informally and amicably disposed of at this point were those of the Postal Telegraph Co., at Detroit, and the International Shoe Co. If the employer, however, refuses to comply with the Board's request to clean house, the regional director next issues a complaint citing in detail the unfair practices with which he is charged.

If the employer still refuses to bring himself within the Board's interpretation of the law, he is given a limited length of time in which to answer the complaint, and a hearing is scheduled before a trial examiner appointed by the Washington office. This differentiation between the prosecuting and investigating functions of the Board, which are handled by members of the regional staff, and the judicial function, handled by Washington, is deliberate. It is a practical way of avoiding unintentional collusion between Board attorneys and Board examiners. At the hearing (only some 5 per cent of all cases so far closed ever reached this stage) the employer may call his witnesses and cross-examine witnesses for the Board; and any labor unions interested in the controversy may intervene. Among others the Borden Co. case, involving some $35,000 in back pay to discharged employees, was settled during the hearing. Following the hearing the trial examiner usually files what is known as an "intermediate report," and everyone concerned is given time to file objections. The report and the objections are reviewed first by the Board's own review section in Washington and finally by the Board itself. The employer may as a rule argue his case orally. A number of companies have been given a clean bill of health upon review—among them the Solvay Process Co., the United Fruit Co., and the General Chemical Co.; and substantial portions of other complaints have been dismissed. But as industry contends, only a few cases are dismissed in full after a hearing. If the Board finds the employer guilty as charged, he is again urged to bring himself within the law without further litigation. If he refuses, the Board then petitions a circuit court of appeals for a court order directing the employer to conform with the Board's cease-and-desist order. At this time the employer has the right to have his case reviewed by a court. It is only when the circuit court of appeals upholds the Board's order—it may be from one to more than two years after the filing of the original charge—that the employer comes under legal compulsion to obey the law. His only further appeal is to the Supreme Court. . . .

The purpose of all so-called labor legislation is to equalize to some degree the bargaining powers of the employer and employee. The late Chief Justice Taft, of the Supreme Court of the U.S., in a decision in 1921, defined the need for unionization perhaps as effectively as it has ever been expressed: "They [labor unions] were organized out of the necessities of the situation. A single employee was helpless in dealing with an employer. He was dependent ordinarily on his daily wage for the maintenance of himself and family. If the employer refused to pay him the wages that he thought fair, he was nevertheless unable to leave the employ and to resist arbitrary and unfair treatment. Union was essential to give laborers opportunity to deal on equality with their employer. They united to exert influence upon him and to leave him in a body in order by this inconvenience to induce him to make better terms with them. They were withholding their labor of economic value to make him pay what they thought it was worth. The right to combine for such a lawful purpose has in many years not been denied by any court."

The National Labor Relations Act in its present form for the first time in the history of the U.S. assures labor a right that, as Mr. Justice Taft said, "has in many years not been denied by any court." It does that successfully; it does very little more: but that it should be fully empowered to do if it is to remain the law of the land.

The New Deal at the Polls

How then, as Roosevelt's second term drew toward a close, did the American people regard the New Deal? One means of measurement was the letters they wrote to Washington; another was their response when they went to the polls in 1940 to vote for or against Roosevelt for an unprecedented third term.

✔ 17. Johnston Avery, "(Signed) The Forgotten Man." *Johnston Avery, "(Signed) The Forgotten Man," Forum (June 1939), 330-334. Reprinted by permission.*

This is an article by a thousand authors. A thousand different persons, residing in forty-two different States, have contributed to its preparation.

Each of these was concerned over the affairs of the government.

Each had something to say. Each had some very definite conviction as to what ought or ought not to be done. Each was sufficiently aroused to sit down and write his views to Robert H. Jackson, Solicitor General of the United States. And I have been in Mr. Jackson's mailbag. I have just read a thousand letters.

The issue raised was the one issue which seems to arouse the people most today. Partisans would state it in different forms. One would ask: Are the practices of big business dangerous to the continuance of small independent industry? Another would inquire: Is the Administration stirring up class war by arraying the masses against those who employ labor? And each would answer: Yes.

That was the question, in whatever form you wish to put it, which inspired these thousand letters. Yet it is not the number who favored or opposed which interests me. There is neither enlightenment nor dependability in a mathematical poll of that sort. It is the state of mind of each group that seems important. What do they think and how intensely do they think it? That is important to know.

These letters fell naturally into three piles, each distinctive of one school of thought. In the first pile were placed the letters from opponents of the Administration; in the second pile were letters from persons who supported the Administration but were primarily interested in some plan of their own; and in the third pile were letters of enthusiastic support. The obviously crank letters were thrown out altogether.

The opponents of the Administration did not provide any thought which had not previously appeared in the press. To reproduce in detail the arguments they used would be to reproduce what most of us have already read. A summary will suffice.

An amazingly large number were personally abusive of the man to whom they wrote. They thought he was insincere, that his only motive was to win votes, that he would actually endanger civilization to snare an office for himself. The "you have never met a payroll" argument was the most popular verbal club with which to beat him over the head.

Next came the contention that the Administration's fight on business is driving down stocks and thus dissipating the income of widows and orphans. Cases were cited wherein a declining market, resulting from "this attack on business," was causing suffering. One doctor wrote that a patient was apt to die as a result and "I shall consider you largely responsible for his death."

The lack of an Administration policy was the third most popular argument. We don't need to spend much time reviewing that contention, since the editorial writers and commentators have left nothing to be said. The policy under the NRA was contrasted with the newer policy of an antimonopoly drive, with what appeared to the writers to be with devastating effect. "What is poor business to do in the face of this pepper-box policy which is apt to shake out anything," cried one man whose sentiments are shared by many.

Next came the affirmation of faith in business leaders. These particular writers would prefer to follow the leadership of certain big businessmen rather than the leadership of those now in charge of the government. This nation, they contend, has been made what it is by the genius of its great business leaders, and it will be wrecked, if it is wrecked, by the leadership of government officials unskilled in business.

A small, but yet amazing, number believe that the President and his advisers are deliberately attempting to undermine the American system. And there are always the extremists, usually anonymous, who say the President is crazy and is trying to set himself up as a dictator.

There is no desire to dismiss the arguments against the Administration, but at the same time there is no need to repeat arguments grown familiar with use.

From the point of interest, therefore, let us get to the views of the voiceless masses, who, from this sample expression, seem to be supporting the Administration.

That statement is made after considerable thought. The views of these people are not found in any major newspaper that I read. They are not found anywhere except in the letters from these people themselves. It may explain many things, not the least of which is the action of prominent public officials. Certainly a leftish advocate is not wanting for encouragement, even though every editorial page in the country lampoons him from morning until night. Those who would understand the sentiment in this country might profit by reading the mail which pours in on spokesmen for the Administration viewpoint. No one could read those thousand letters or, I venture to say, any thousand letters which similarly boil from the public, without reaching the firm conviction that a majority of the masses is restless for change.

After reading for several days I devised a formula which seemed uncannily accurate. If the letter had been dictated on lithographed or engraved stationery, the chances were about 75 to 25 that it opposed the Administration. If it had been personally pecked out on a typewriter, the chances of criticism or support were about 50-50, and the same division applied to what might be termed finishing-school- or college-handwriting letters. But, if the letter had been written in pencil and on tablet paper, the chances were about 99 to 1 that the writer was a staunch supporter of the Administration.

These are the people who don't write letters to the editors. They have no faith in their literary ability, but, when a wholesale attack is made on policies which they approve, they are moved to express their approbation to the man thus attacked. Most of them, recognizing that they are voiceless, take great pains to tell that a poll of sentiment in their humble parlor or at the country store or in a particular group of workmen developed the information that every person thus polled expressed similar support.

These are mere facts—cold, bald, unvarnished facts; and the thousand letters may be produced to substantiate them. The only point of dispute is on the question of how representative of the thought of the nation are these thousand letters. I believe they are representative and I believe any other thousand letters similarly inspired would produce the same picture.

Now let us see what these voiceless persons who write on tablet paper with pencils are thinking.

First, we can set down four broad general impressions which are inescapable from a reading of this mail.

1. These people will not stand another depression, and they have no faith in the ability of so-called big businessmen to prevent one. They think too much greed by a few persons is causing too much suffering among many persons.

2. What they want most of all is *security* of income rather than *amount* of income. It is the uncertainty, the constant prospect of family suffering, which is driving them to the point of desperation. They think the system should provide work for those willing to work. Even though they presently have jobs, they live in constant fear of being laid off.

3. They think the newspapers represent big business and that public leaders should use the radio more and more. They depend to an astonishing extent on the radio for their information.

4. If the Roosevelt reforms fail, these people are ready to follow a leadership far more to the left. Another Huey Long could win support unknown to the late Louisiana dictator. Unless the Roosevelt program is able to bring about some measure of the social security they are demanding, they will call for such a leader.

Any person who makes those statements, even though he collects them from a thousand authors, will be charged with stirring up class war, breeding revolution, arraying labor against capital, and advocating a regime of socialism. One could almost write in advance the letters he will receive from indignant citizens.

The answer is that any effort to prevent those unpleasant things must be made by facing facts; that we cannot stop the explosion of a powder keg by blindly denying the existence of a powder keg. It is there, just as certainly as some social reform is certain. "It will come either by an orderly process or by a disorderly process," says one spokesman of a large group whose power of expression is more cryptic than that of his fellow men. But come it surely will.

There are several pertinent and little recognized facts, all culled from these "unthinking" masses, which have a direct bearing on this situation. Perhaps we should back up a bit and let some of them set the stage for this apparent change in our political life.

Twenty-five years ago this nation was turning out less than 200,000 high-school graduates a year, and almost 8 per cent of the population were illiterate. Now we are turning out over a million high-school graduates a year, and barely 2 per cent of the population are illiterate. With the ability to read, there inevitably comes an ability to think, points out a Midwestern farmer. And thinking is naturally tuned to the environments in which one is forced to think, adds a twenty-seven-year-old lawyer from Texas. To expect a man who lives in the uncertainty of hand-to-mouth existence to think in terms of Park Avenue is as shortsighted, says a New England bank clerk, as the admonition to let them eat cake when the bread is gone.

Twenty-five years ago there were no radios in this country. Now there are being sold about nine million sets a year, and there must be approximately twenty or twenty-five million sets in use. As never before, points out an eighty-year-old man from Brooklyn, public leaders can figuratively sit down in the living rooms of the entire nation and discuss with the citizens the affairs of the government. "And the masses stay home to listen while Park Avenue goes to a party," he thinks.

Such a development as that of radio must inevitably have a far-reaching effect on the electorate of the nation.

Its obvious effect "is to organize the masses," points out one man from the masses in Seattle. If any proof of that is required, we can find it readily in the last *Literary Digest* presidential poll. In previous years that poll had been accurate even to fractional degrees. It was conducted the same way in 1936, but those who formerly had controlled elections in their various communities found themselves snowed under by an organized but voiceless mass who, perhaps, "will control more and more the elections in this country," says another New Yorker.

We cannot have under the same roof an educated public with intimate communications on the one hand and obvious social and economic injustices on the other, according to a large but bad-spelling group.

No longer may any leader win election to high public office who does not speak the voice of the voiceless millions. Call that an advocacy of demagoguery if you will, but the very system which we have nursed through the generations "has brought it about," believe others.

We wanted public education, so "now we must adjust our government to best serve the needs of an educated nation," says a man from the South who pecks it out on a typewriter. We wanted mass production of radio and automobiles, so now we must meet the exactions of a mass public welded together by such ready means of communication, think many more. We wanted to build our standard of living up to the place where it would create a rich market for our manufactured products, so now we must go forward with the imposed doctrine that the laboring class is entitled to the comforts of life. "We cannot tell a child it must grow only so large and then must stop growing," is an expression from one of the political adolescents. If we do not wish it to become a full grown man, it is best "not to nurse it so tenderly in the infancy."

The masses of America are now politically full grown, "and getting stronger every day." No more do they have to labor through the ordeal of reading what somebody else says a public leader said a week or a month ago. Now they sit back in their favorite chairs and hear with their own ears, says another, "the words as they come from the lips of our public leaders."

And the problems most important to them are the problems which mostly affect them—security of jobs or security of price for the things they grow, security against the crushing misery of old age, security of their dignity as American citizens, security against the unspeakable disgrace of begging in vain for an opportunity to support their families. Those are the things they have been taught to expect. Those are the things they are going to demand.

Whether we like it or not, whether it is wise or not, whether it is dangerous or not, "a new condition of political life has arrived," says one labor leader. The masses are organized, repeat many others. Their broad problems are identical. Their environments are similar. "They think as a group, and they are going to vote as a group," think others. And theirs "is the power to elect or defeat," believe many of these writers.

To realize that and attempt to supply the demands intelligently is to render a service to the American people and their traditions. To deny it and seek to block a democratic majority "is to endanger democracy itself," according to a resolution passed by a labor union on the West Coast.

We cannot adjust the thinking of a nation, believes a small businessman, to suit the practices "of business or even the traditions of America." Instead, the reverse is true. All else "must be adjusted to fit the thinking of the nation." It will be adjusted. It is only a question "of how that adjustment will come." It will come by intelligent leadership from the top or else it will come by a more rowdy method from the masses, warn many. Neither course is likely to be perfect in the beginning. The first would be safer. The second—and we may as well face it—is tending toward a demand that "the government take over all banks, insurance companies, and public utilities," according to a spokesman for an astonishingly large school of thought.

"Why," asks one man whose thoughts are identical with many others, "should the government pay interest on money which it owns anyway?" Regardless of the logic we may array in answer to that query, the important fact is that the masses are beginning to demand a more paternalistic government—"and the masses will rule at the ballot box," warns a man who is the secretary of another West Coast labor union.

Our more conservative brothers will demand of us, Why do you put such ideas in the public mind?

That's just it. We are not. These ideas are coming from the public mind, and it is only "a leader with his head buried in the sand" who refuses to recognize them. "We may delay reform but we cannot permanently block it," many are telling us in language which jibes with the thoughts of a writer whose chief grudge is against chain stores.

But what reform can we give without wrecking the capitalistic system?

Plenty. "The first task is to reform our own thinking," cautions a moderately well-known college professor.

An old-age pension was considered the extreme of radical and irrational thought when first suggested. Not even the high-placed leftish advocates would come close to it. Is it really dangerous? Let's see.

"There are only approximately ten million persons in the United States who are over sixty years of age. Surely some principle of insurance could be devised to protect these citizens against the ravages of a dependent old age," believes one letter writer, a man who is in the early thirties.

There are many prospects, many ways of making it practical. The chief obstacle in the way "is our state of mind, our national conservatism which forbids the entertainment of any new suggestion or reform until the force of conditions" leaves no alternative, says another. For the preservation of what we call "our liberties" we think nothing of spending billions in "preparing for war to kill ourselves and others" who might threaten our industrial life, "but we shudder in amazement at the suggestion of spending a like amount to *save* the lives of those who have poured their blood and energies into the building up of this nation," ridicules still another who is himself economically safe at present.

From these thousand letters you could lay in one pile approximately 600 which agreed on one thought: that the door of opportunity for the little man is being closed. They do not all agree on the cause nor do they all agree on the remedy. But there is an ominous unanimity on the fact.

Mathematically, there is one other interesting development. A vast majority of young men and a vast majority of old men are supporting the Administration. On the one hand they see no opportunity ahead; on the other hand they have seen a life of work gone to the enrichment of others than themselves.

The views of the young, however, seemed most interesting.

"I am a college graduate, says one typical letter, "and I have now reached the conclusion that I could have better spent those four years learning some manual trade." Still another warns of "a restlessness among the coming generation not realized by those in secure positions." A man from Dallas writes, on crest-embossed stationery, that people are being educated to the fact that "fair practices ultimately bring the best result"; and another from Cheyenne says that "90 per cent of our political leaders are definitely under the influence of organized business."

"We do not want Communism or Socialism or any other ism," writes a twenty-nine-year-old former newspaperman, "but unless big business becomes less selfish we are going to be forced to join any movement which promises to break up the system which we feel is crushing us."

If it is a choice between dictatorship and a "continuance of economic slavery," writes a clerk in a large corporation, "we will take dictatorship." We will "take anything," he adds, "and I know the people who work around me feel the same way I do. We can't talk, but O Boy, we can vote." All they want, he said, is the right leader "because President Roosevelt is too big hearted to really crack down on the fellows who are cracking down on us." The President doesn't know what it is to be at the "mercy of a heartless company which, to protect its own fat dividends and executives' salaries, can," with merely a little slip of yellow paper, "cause my children to go hungry and miserable."

There is no purpose in continuing further. The picture of this state of mind among the masses could be enlarged but could not be made any sharper. How representative is it? Only a relative answer will suffice. Conditions could make it grow worse; other conditions could make it grow less.

And the astounding, the encouraging, thing about this state of mind is the fact that the masses thus represented do not want to depart from the traditional American system. They think they may have to, but they would much prefer to find some way to make our present system work.

This, it seems to many Americans, is the most engaging challenge ever presented to this country.

18. Samuel Lubell, "Post-Mortem: Who Elected Roosevelt?"

When Roosevelt won re-election to a third term after a stiffly contested campaign against the Republican nominee, Wendell Willkie, Samuel Lubell surveyed thirteen American cities for the *Saturday Evening Post* to try to determine why Roosevelt had won. In so doing, he set forth also the way in which the New Deal had changed the lives and attitudes of large groups of people in these cities. His survey (with some deletions) follows. *Samuel Lubell, "Post-Mortem: Who Elected Roosevelt?"* Saturday Evening Post (*January 25, 1941*), 9-11, 91-96. *Reprinted by permission.*

Much more than the third-term tradition was shattered when President Roosevelt took the oath of office again on Monday.

Who elected him? As in all elections, there were many crosscurrents, but the 1940 answer is simple and inescapable.

The little fellow elected him, because there are more of the little fellow and because he believed Mr. Roosevelt to be his friend and protector.

Roosevelt won by the vote of labor, unorganized as well as organized, plus that of the foreign born and their first and second generation descendants. And the Negro.

It was a class-conscious vote for the first time in American history, and the implications are portentous. The New Deal appears to have accomplished what the Socialists, the I.W.W. and the Communists never could approach. It has drawn a class line across the face of American politics. That line seems to be there to stay. While thousands of wage earners, even voters on relief, voted for Willkie, we are talking here about groups as wholes.

Mr. Roosevelt is the first President to owe his election in such great measure to the teeming cities. On the farms and in the towns Mr. Willkie more than held his own. It was in the industrial centers that the Republican hopes were blacked out in factory smoke.

The Republican campaign had virtually no effect on this vote, the evidence argues. I doubt that anything Willkie might have done would have affected it. The election was not decided on the issues he debated, but on forces long at work—economic status, nationalities, birth rates. The rise of government as an employer on a scale rivaling the biggest business is a fourth. And the indications are that this vote might have gone to Roosevelt for a fourth or a fifth term as readily as for a third.

It is an American habit to forget an election quickly when the votes have been counted. We did so, as usual, and, so, few yet have grasped the fact that this was not just another election. The Republicans do not know what hit them; the Democrats, certainly as distinguished from the New Dealers, do not know what they hit the Republicans with. The New Deal has aimed at a bloodless revolution.

In 1940 it went a long way toward accomplishing it.

In numbers it was no great victory. Roosevelt won by the smallest plurality and the smallest percentage of the total vote since the neck-and-neck election of 1916. If his strength should diminish between now and 1944 at the same rate it did between 1936 and 1940, he would be beaten in 1944.

The opposition is taking comfort in these figures, but the 1940 vote upset the fundamentals of our old two-party system, and when the fundamentals are overturned, past-performance figures are worthless.

In considerable measure the vote was personal for Mr. Roosevelt. No one may say how far, if he does not run for a fourth term, he might be able to deliver this vote in 1944 to an heir. What is clear is that, once Roosevelt is out of the picture, this vote will not slip back automatically into its former slots. The political wars henceforth will be fought with new tactics and new weapons to unpredictable results.

I say this on the basis of a firsthand study of thirteen of the cities, from Boston to Seattle, which piled up the Roosevelt vote. While the body still was warm, the *Post* sent me to hold a post-mortem. My instructions were:

"Ignore the Solid South and the machine vote. Stay out of actual slums; these may be taken for granted. Forget the rights and wrongs of the campaign. Something extraordinary happened on November fifth. Find out where the rest of the New Deal vote came from, and why. Then tell your findings as impartially as if you were reporting a football game."

In thirteen large cities I studied the returns by wards, then by precincts, then by neighborhoods. When I had winnowed out the less significant, I went on foot into the others, talking to ward leaders and precinct captains, to churchmen, union officials, businessmen, and housewives. In each city I concentrated finally upon a sample which best seemed to reflect that city as a whole—in Boston, an Irish ward; in Detroit, an automobile workers' district.

BOSTON.

In the shadow of the Bunker Hill Monument, in historic Charlestown, Roosevelt rolled up a plurality of nearly four to one. The frame houses built in the days of Edward Everett still stand. Mounting the narrow hillside streets to the monument, they seem heaped one on top of another in factory-district congestion, the back yards barely providing clothesline space. Living in those homes today are longshoremen, foundry workers, packers, waitresses, and minor city employees. About 65 per cent are Irish Catholic.

A typical Boston working-class district, Charlestown is not a slum. Poorer sections of the city went nine to one for Roosevelt. Prevailing incomes of Charlestown families range from $1,200 to $1,500; about one in five own their homes. Those who do are mighty proud of it. Good-sized metal plates proclaiming the owner's name are nailed to every door like family shields.

William J. Galvin, the thirty-six-year-old councilman and Democratic ward leader, has a simple explanation for the Roosevelt vote: "Probably no section in the country gained more under the New Deal." Galvin can check off the gains against the total ward population of 30,000: hundreds got pay raises under the wage-hour law; more hundreds of seasonal workers are having slack months cushioned by unemployment-insurance benefits. The NYA is helping from 300 to 500 youths; at the worst of the depression thousands held WPA jobs; of 1,500 persons past sixty-five in the ward more than 600 receive old-age assistance; another 600 cases are on direct relief and get aid for dependent children. Charlestown is a food-stamp area; the WPA improved its bathing beach; a new low-cost housing project will relieve some of the ward's congestion.

Nearly one half of those of voting age are under forty. The economic memories of many of these voters begin with Hoover. Galvin's two younger brothers got out of high school during the depression and went into CCC camps. They are now working as electrician's and pipefitter's helpers in the nearby Boston Navy Yard, which has more than quadrupled its employment in recent months. Galvin has two other brothers, a lawyer and a school custodian; one of his brothers-in-law works as a planner in the navy yard and the others work as bookbinder, salesman, and chauffeur. Of nine Galvin breadwinners, five rely on public employment. To the two younger brothers, the New Deal has meant advancement as real as any they could have got under a private employer.

To Charlestown's Irish, the New Deal has meant an advance along other fronts too. They are the sons and daughters, the grandsons and granddaughters of the immigrants who swarmed into Boston in the last quarter of the nineteenth century. Then the "Yankee vote" ruled Massachusetts. Classified-job advertisements carried notices, "No Irish need apply."

But the immigrant Irish reared larger families than the Yankees. Through sheer numbers, they toppled the barriers in profession after profession. By the 20's they had acquired local political dominance. Being Democrats under Republican presidents, though, they were denied federal recognition until Roosevelt.

Reporters in the Boston Federal Building cannot recall a single Irishman on the U.S. district court before 1933. Roosevelt has made the appointments to that court, the names Sweeney and Ford. Postmaster Peter Hague, who lives in Charlestown, is Irish, as are the collector of customs, the U.S. Marshal, several assistant U.S. attorneys. In Charlestown alone, Galvin estimates, Irishmen have got more than 400 federal jobs under the New Deal. Not only for the poor but for those better off economically, Roosevelt has become the champion of the Irish climb up the American ladder. . . .

DETROIT.

Roosevelt's greatest pluralities in Wayne County were registered in the Polish districts of Hamtramck, where precincts went twenty and thirty to one for him. More typical of the city as a whole, though, are two auto-workers precincts in the twenty-first ward which went for Roosevelt three to one.

Economically, these precincts fall into the great average sectors of Detroit. They are a food-stamp area; incomes run between $1,200 and $1,400 a year; neighborhood movies charge 20 cents admission; the well-kept private homes are worth between $2,500 and $5,000. "Sleeping room for rent" signs in many of the windows mirror the transient, half-boom, half-broke nature of auto-plant employment.

Workers in the two precincts are predominantly native white, better than half Protestant. In a random apartment house one finds such names as Baldwin, Walsh, Gibson, Calhoun, Costello, Powers, Snyder, Saltzgiver, and Solomon. Perhaps a fourth of the workers came up from the South during the 20's. Labor says that these "hillbillies," as they are known, were brought in because it was felt that they would be less inclined to join unions and would be easier to handle. Today the hillbillies are high in union councils.

Chrysler Local Seven, in the fore of the sit-down strike of 1937, has its headquarters in one precinct. The local has its own three-floor building, which at shift time becomes a buzz of activity. Four girls behind teller windows collect dues—the local claims 10,000 members. A stream of visitors pours in and out of the offices of the president and the shop committee.

Nearly fifty such United Auto Workers locals are scattered throughout the city. Their listings in the telephone book run to half a column. Only the state, federal, and municipal governments have longer listings. Like many another union, the UAW has become a big business, with its own white-collar opportunities. A stenographer working at Chrysler Seven is the daughter of an auto worker; the educational director is a young man in his thirties, fresh out of the plant. He still wears a work shirt and lumber jacket, but he sits at a desk with a telephone and a buzzer.

Even more so than with the Irish in Boston, Roosevelt, to these auto workers, is the "friend" who gave them recognition. The New Deal enabled them to build their union. It taught them the strength of their numbers and with the feeling of power has come a growing class-consciousness. The workers themselves use the phrase. "I'm franker than you," one local official replied when I asked him why he voted for Roosevelt. "I'll say it, even though it doesn't sound nice. We've grown class-conscious."

A Catholic priest in the precinct confessed, "If I ever attacked Roosevelt from the pulpit, it would be the end of me here."

Listening to these auto workers, one got the feeling that nothing Willkie could have said or done would have changed these votes. John L. Lewis had no effect. In their minds the cleavage between workingman and "economic royalist" is sharply drawn. One also got the feeling that, given the same choice, these workers would vote again and again for Roosevelt, regardless of whether it was the third, fourth or fifth term. . . .

LOS ANGELES.

Even where organized labor still is battling for a foothold, Roosevelt's appeal to the workingman proved overwhelming. Los Angeles has long been known as "open shop." In 1928 Hoover carried the city's fifth district handily; Roosevelt swept it by three to one in 1940.

The skilled craftsmen in the metal and building trades who live here belong to the AFofL. The great mass of unskilled and semiskilled workers remain unorganized, although the CIO is winning adherents. Two rubber factories are located near the district; in one the United Rubber Workers have a contract. A near-by steel mill has signed with the CIO.

Save for a few apartment houses the district is composed of small homes, mainly frame bungalows. About 40 per cent are owned by the workers; rents for the others run from $20 to $30. Rents are low in Los Angeles, and this area falls in the middle third for the city. About one fourth of the families earn less than $1,800; the others up to $2,500.

MINNEAPOLIS.

"Traditionally Republican" is the political label still applied to both Minneapolis and Minnesota. In 1938 youthful Harold Stassen broke the Farmer-Labor hold. In 1940, political experts reasoned, the pendulum would continue its swing back to "normal" Republicanism. To their surprise, Roosevelt carried the city by 17,000, the state by 47,000. What happened to the pendulum?

As in every city sampled, Minneapolis's vote broke primarily along economic lines. In the seven lowest-income wards, with rentals averaging under $30 a month, Roosevelt won by better than two and a half to one. In the four wards with rentals from $30 to $40 a month, it was Roosevelt by seven to six. In the three wards where the rental average topped $40, Willkie won by five to three. Roosevelt managed to squeeze through in one of these three wards by 8,251 to 8,066. In the highest-income ward, Willkie's margin fell just under three to one.

One ward which helped check the pendulum's swing was the tenth, where the late Floyd Olson, the Farmer-Labor leader, lived. A newer residential district lying near the north end of town, the ward scales about halfway on Minneapolis' economic ladder. It scores seventh in relief cases; average in department-store deliveries; better than average in automobiles owned.

In the precinct sampled, where Roosevelt led by two to one, virtually all the families own their homes. Mainly frame-and-stucco dwellings with sun-parlor porches, they fall into the FHA value range, from $4,000 to $7,000. Most incomes run between $1,800 and $2,500, with a goodly number of workers earning better than $3,000.

High-school education for the children is about universal; college rare. Roughly 70 per cent are of Norwegian or Swedish descent, the dominant nationalities in the city. Sympathy for Norway helped Roosevelt.

Minneapolis is an AFofL union city and probably 80 per cent of the workers in the precinct are unionized. Major occupations are the metal and building trades, trucking and driving milk wagons. Truckers and milk drivers belong to the Teamsters Union, which is popularly credited with running City Hall.

Roosevelt made his first campaign speech before the Teamsters Convention in Washington, reminding the union of its progress in membership under the New Deal, from 70,000 to 400,000. The Teamsters needed little reminding. Like the railroaders, they went down the line for their "friend" in the White House. The head of one precinct church with a number of teamsters in his congregation was outspoken in condemning the third term. He admitted bitterly, "I don't suppose I changed a single vote."

As a footnote to the pendulum mystery, some birth-rate statistics can be cited. They show two great waves of births, the first between 1890 and 1900, when the Scandinavians poured into the city, almost quadrupling the population; the second, between 1911 and 1920, when the children of those immigrants began bearing offspring. From that second wave have been coming the new voters. If Minneapolis continues to vote on economic lines, the future looks black for the Republicans. In 1937 a Minneapolis Council of Social Agencies study revealed that virtually all neighborhoods with 30 per cent or more of the population under fifteen—the future voters—were "proletarian or middle class." The "gold coasts" had 15 per cent of their population under fifteen years of age.

PHILADELPHIA.

Pennsylvania, too, was classed as a pendulum state. Black Republican by tradition, the state returned to the party in 1938. In Philadelphia, to boot, the mayor was Republican. Yet Roosevelt swept the city by 177,000.

What seems to have happened emerges most clearly in the twenty-second ward. Both in 1938 and in 1940 the Republican vote stood at 31,000. Roosevelt, though, ran 6,000 votes better than did the Democrats in 1938. His vote of 20,000 was as great as in his record year of 1936. Whatever Roosevelt lost because of the third term was more than made up from new voters.

In the first precinct, which Roosevelt carried nearly two to one, he increased his 1936 plurality. It is a typical Roosevelt neighborhood, with rentals ranging from $30 to $45 a month. Even after 1932 the precinct registered overwhelmingly Republican; now the Democrats have a slight edge.

Ward Committeeman Vincent Dean went down the precinct voters' list. He picked out twenty-four families where someone had got a government job since the New Deal; this out of about 450 families. He checked off the new Democratic registrants—thirty-four, with twenty-four of them women. One, a seventy-year-old woman who receives a pension from the government, had never voted before in her life. Two had recently been naturalized; a third had come up from North Carolina. Three women were got out by their union-member husbands, a railroad man, a machinist, a cloth weaver.

We checked the list for the size of families. The Republicans had twenty-three households with three or more voters; the Democrats had forty-three. Since Roosevelt ran ahead of the Democratic registration, he may have got some of those big Republican families. One Democratic family, running through three generations, had fourteen voters. Two had been added in November.

CHICAGO.

Here, as expected, can be found the smoothest-working ward machine in the country. In the twenty-fourth ward, Jake Arvey, No. 3 man in the Kelly-Nash organization, delivered for Roosevelt 26,314 to 1,918. Of greater significance for our national cross-section is a little precinct in the comfortably residential fortieth ward.

When Caleb Enix, who sits in the slot of the copy desk on the Chicago *Daily News,* moved into the precinct more than twenty years ago, it was overwhelmingly Republican. Perhaps twenty Democratic votes out of 400. For the most part, the same families still live here. They went for Roosevelt three to two.

In a few apartment houses on the corners, rentals run from $35 to $40. The rest of the precinct is made up of home owners. Enix knows each neighbor's business—a landscape gardener, a retired plumber, a minor executive in a lumber company, two post-office employees, a pressman, a teacher, an auto mechanic, a widow with two sons working in Peoria. Incomes range, in the main, between $2,500 and $3,500. Most of the children finish high school; only the exceptions get to college. Asked how much the houses in the precinct are worth, Enix hedges a bit, then puts them at $5,000 to $10,000. The homes are old and wouldn't bring that on the market, but Enix, who is looking forward to retiring, has no intention of selling. And it makes him feel better to think his house is worth more than less.

At the bottom of the depression about half the workers in the precinct were unemployed. Now Enix knows of only one, and he is not in need. Enix's daughter is married; his son, Caleb, Jr., is preparing to work for Uncle Sam as a radio operator.

Caleb, Jr., is twenty-four, and his idea of a good job is based on depression standards. "Any of the fellows around here can make money if they want to," he explains. "I have a friend down the street who's a salesman. He can make $35 a week any time he wants to."

Three banks in the neighborhood failed and almost every family lost part of its savings. Many lost their homes; others were bailed out by the HOLC. One of the shut bank buildings still stands. Its cashier windows are deserted, but the safety-deposit boxes still are used. Enix and his neighbors seem to vote against those deserted cashier windows and for those safety-deposit boxes. To them, Roosevelt means rescued savings and a promise of security.

SEATTLE.

Another middle-class sample of different composition, the Upper Broadway district here is an old, settled neighborhood. Its population is almost exclusively native white. In 1928 it went Hoover two to one; in 1940 Roosevelt by three to two.

Unlike Enix's precinct, it is not a deeply rooted area of family residences. Once the fashionable part of the city, it now is being passed over for the automobile reaches near Lake Washington and the bluff overlooking Puget Sound. Many an old private residence has been converted into a duplex or a rooming house. In the last twenty years a number of medium-priced apartment houses have been erected. Rents average from $30 to $45 a month.

White-collar workers predominate. An afternoon's interviewing yielded a municipal-transit employee, a telephone installer, a salesman, druggist, insurance agent, office manager, longshoreman, real-estate man, teacher, bookkeeper, cashier, and chemist. Their incomes ran from $1,500 to $2,200 a year. The shops in the neighborhood, one and two stories high, fit typical middle-class needs—groceries, bakeries, hamburger spots, restaurants, filling stations, cabinetmakers, tailors. Some storekeepers live over their shops. . . .

BROOKLYN.

From city to city the dividing line fluctuates somewhat. If we think of the economic voting as falling into horizontal strata, then there also have been vertical vote movements cutting across economic lines and lifting the Roosevelt vote. These, naturally, would be most evident in the dividing zones. As major influences of this sort could be listed:

Organized labor reaching up into the better-paid skills.

The government, as an employer sprinkling' jobs through all middle-class groups.

The whole body of New Deal benefits, from relief to FHA mortgages. Precisely in this economic range are New Deal votes thickest.

Nationalistic and religious sympathies stirred by Hitlerism, as with the Jews, the Poles, the Scandinavians, and the Czechs. Where these sympathies coincide with a low economic status as with the Poles, the Roosevelt pluralities are enormous. Where they cut across higher economic rungs, like among better-income Jews, wards normally Republican swing Democratic or have their majorities cut, while Democratic-inclined wards go Roosevelt by land-slide proportions.

In Brooklyn's Eighteenth Assembly District, Roosevelt won by about four to one, for a plurality of 70,000. The neighborhood is 65 per cent Jewish and 25 per cent Irish Catholic. Perhaps one in three is foreign born. There are a few slum shacks; there is a small Negro section; in one corner of the district are walk-up tenements occupied chiefly by needle-trades workers. One-time Socialists, they voted for Roosevelt on the American Labor Party ticket.

But by far the great majority live in one and two family houses worth between $5,000 and $10,000—hundreds of new FHA homes are being built; some 180,000 FHA homes were under way in the nation in 1940—or in modern apartment houses renting for $45 to $65 a month. These apartments have automatic elevators, mechanical refrigerators, tiled bathrooms, walled-in showers and, in most cases, a doorman. He is not the Park Avenue kind. The Eighteenth's doormen are just middle-class, "keeping up with the Joneses" copies. The majority don't have full uniforms, but wear braided jackets over ordinary street trousers.

In the main, we find skilled workers, some professional people, fairly successful salesmen and, the largest category, small businessmen. Most incomes range between $3,000 and $7,000, with the general level of living around $4,000. Even families earning less try to live on that scale. A considerable number of wives work, not because of careers or necessity, but to be able to maintain their "Joneses" living standards.

Mostly, the voters are the sons and daughters—with the second generation coming up—of immigrants. They have risen from poverty. They now are straining to keep their upper-middle-class perch. Few families have more than two children, and the children they have are showered with attention. Babies of carriage age, before being taken into the street—at least twice a day—must be dressed up to pass the competitive inspection of the neighbors. At ten or eleven each morning, in front of any apartment house, the mothers may be seen, clad in fur coats, parading their babies.

Apartments, in general, are three and four rooms, reflecting the predominance of young couples. If the nonworking, elderly group is ruled out, less than thirty-five would be an average age for bread-winners. Many are little businessmen who started in for themselves after 1933. Those who prospered are loud in Roosevelt's praise; the others usually have got along with a struggle. Whether, ultimately, New Deal spending will force a write-off of their savings, thus far those savings have remained intact. Always there is the hope that one good season will ease all the strains.

The fact that most of these people are brothers and sisters in large families and that the fortunes of one member of the family react upon the others must be counted as one of the unseen factors favoring Roosevelt. Simply as a matter of numbers, these families are likely to have some member still struggling up the lower rungs where New Deal benefits are greatest. That would hold true for other middle-class elements—the Irish in Boston, for example. By kinship and immigrant heritage, their sympathies are rooted in the underdog income levels where Roosevelt's appeal is greatest.

St. Louis.

From the 1880's until the depression, the great industrial cities were magnets drawing in excess populations. The cities drew not only from abroad but from within our own borders, from the Midwest and South. St. Louis, for example, has only 10 per cent foreign born in its population. Yet here, too, we find the same inexorable spread of numbers, the same leveling that is going on in the other cities sampled.

Republicans, with the aid of the automobile, have been abandoning St. Louis for the suburbs. In 1932 Roosevelt carried St. Louis County—the city vote is excluded—by 23,000. In his record-breaking year of 1936 his plurality dropped to 17,000. By last November enough Republicans had been transplanted for Willkie to win the county by 15,000. St. Louis city has become almost entirely working class. Roosevelt took every ward but one where there happens to be a strong Negro Republican machine.

Perhaps the last outposts of St. Louis' vanishing Republicans lie in the twenty-eighth ward, the old silk-stocking district. In 1932, the GOP carried the ward; in November they held only three precincts. Along Lindell Boulevard and Skinker Road, the old, imposing homes still stand, mansion-like in design, with graveled driveways, flagstone walks, antique-fabricated lampposts, spreading trees and spacious lawns. On many a lawn and tree, though, is a "for sale" sign.

All through the swankier streets homes are for sale. Apartments which once brought $125 a month now go for $60 and $75; homes that cost $50,000 have been halved in price, though the ward still is as creamy a residential district as there is in the city.

Fine old residences are being razed to make way for apartments. Along Delmar Boulevard the beauty parlors are cutting prices; a custom-built upholsterer advertises an "income purchase plan."

Once, at the Pageant Theater, the neighborhood movie, seats were reserved. Now, on Wednesdays and Thursdays double features are shown for 15 cents; on Fridays and Saturdays three features for a quarter.

HARLEM.

How great has been the impact of this urban revolt upon the traditional Republican line-up can be seen in the Negro vote. Only in St. Louis, which continues to draw them from the South, do the Negroes still seem divided in their allegiances between the party of Lincoln and the party of Roosevelt. Harlem's Seventeenth Assembly District went better than seven to one for the New Deal.

Probably 50 per cent of Harlem's Negroes are getting relief of some kind. Older Negroes—they're most likely to be Republican—shake their graying heads ruefully and mutter, "Our people are selling their birthrights for a mess of pottage."

To the younger Negroes the WPA and relief mean not only material aid but a guaranty that no longer must they work at any salary given them, that they are entitled—they emphasize the word—to a living wage. Through the WPA, Harlem's Negroes have had opened to them white-collar opportunities which before had been shut, such as the music and art and writers' projects. Negroes, too, remember that Mrs. Roosevelt visited Harlem personally, that President Roosevelt has appointed more Negroes to administrative positions paying around $5,000 a year than any President before him. Each time Roosevelt makes such an appointment, the *Amsterdam News,* Harlem's leading newspaper, headlines it in 72-point type. Every young Negro gets a vicarious thrill thinking, "There may be a chance up there for me."

Harlem definitely has grown class as well as race conscious. Last year the Seventeenth for the first time got a Negro installed as Democratic leader of the district. Under the warming hand of the great white father in Washington a flock of unions has sprung up. They include garment workers, janitors, bartenders, waitresses, waiters, Pullman porters, laundry workers, newspapermen, retail clerks, and redcaps.

Consumer and tenant leagues have arisen to battle with Harlem's disgraceful housing problem. All sorts of groups are pressing campaigns to force neighborhood stores, once manned entirely by whites, to hire Negroes. Initiated after a race riot a few years ago the drive has met with astonishing success.

Today, Negroes work in hundreds of establishments as behind-the-counter salesmen, as movie cashiers, as meat cutters, as sales-girls in department stores. Some labor groups hold daily classes to teach Negroes selling, typing, and stenography. This is done so that the unions will be able to rebuff employers who protest, "I can't hire Negroes; they're not experienced." The proportion of Negro-owned stores is growing.

Whether or not Roosevelt is responsible, he gets the credit. In many a Harlem home hangs a rotogravure photograph of the new emancipator; some families have spent 50 cents to have it framed.

A young police reporter on the *News* summed it up when he remarked, "Negroes feel Roosevelt started something."

"Something" certainly has been started. In 1932 Roosevelt became President in a popular recoil against the depression. His third-term victory, however, is the result of an upsurging of the urban masses. In the New Deal they have found their leveling philosophy; under it they have been given recognition through patronage, benefits, and new opportunities; they have been awakened to the consciousness of the power of their numbers.